Color my Style

Discover the uniqueness in You!

ANGELA "KITTY" DAILY

COLOR MY STYLE
Discover The Uniqueness In You!

Angela "Kitty" Daily
angela.daily@sbcglobal.net

Copyright © 2022
ISBN 978-1-943343-32-4

Destined To Publish
destinedtopublish.com | 773-783-2981

Acknowledgments

"I can do all things through Christ which strengtheneth me" (Philippians 4:13, KJV).

I never imagined, fantasized, or dreamed it could be a reality for me to write a book. But guess what? I did it! Honestly, this has never been on my bucket list, but in pandemic times, God uncovered this gift and showed me there's more to give. I believe there are additional hidden talents and gifts waiting to be revealed.

I dedicate this book first and foremost to my Lord and Savior Jesus Christ, who allowed me to be in the place where He ordained and planned for me to endure these breathtaking experiences. I thought on many occasions about turning around and giving up, but instead my experiences boosted me to unimaginable freedom. Freedom to stand, freedom to be bold and speak truth to any situation without intentional hurt or harm to anyone. Freedom to be authentically me.

I also dedicate it to my parents, Mayfield and Earnestine Hall, who set my sister and me up for success and denied themselves so we could be exposed to the best they could offer and afford. I say thank you for your love and support. We miss you dearly and hope you are gazing down from heaven with smiles on your faces.

To my one and only sister, May Hall-Anastascio. We were taught to excel and not to be intimidated by anyone or anything. God has blessed us beyond measure. I can always count on you to be my biggest supporter and ally. You will always be my shero.

To family and friends. Thank you for your reinforcement, support, and love.

A special thank you to Reverend Stephanie Bradley, facilitator at the testing center in Illinois, who spoke the words to me as I came out of the exam room where I failed the test. You looked at me and said with sincerity and intensity, "So, when are you going to write that book?"

I laughed and thought, what is wrong with this lady?

You then proceeded to tell me, "You have something to tell the world."

My eyes were opened at that very moment and I understood the missing piece that I hadn't been able to find in the entrepreneurial vision given to me in 2015. It took five years for God to show me the next segment of the dream during an uncompromising pandemic in 2020. What I learned was patience and the importance of never giving up hope that the dream would come with permission to move forward when God gave the green light to go.

To Pastor T.D. Jakes of the Potter's House. We pressed through some of the worst times in our history in the year 2020. It was your anointed virtual Sunday services and Wednesday Bible classes that encouraged and strengthened me to press on despite the grim conditions. We had to tolerate the position we were placed in, a cave like the one Elijah ran to for refuge, insulated and isolated so God could speak to us alone. But we knew with assurance that when we eventually came out of that cave, we would not be the same and God would bring us before great kings. It was in the cave that new gifts were revealed.

To Pastor Dr. E. Dewey Smith of The House of Hope. Thank you for Morning Dew on Tuesday and for Thursday morning Bible class. How grateful I am for your vision of Hope TV that aided in sustaining me and so many others during the pandemic and beyond. Such great teaching, so much concern for our well-being, and such great wisdom were extended to the listeners.

To the Destined Publishing staff. Thank you for the patience, guidance, and support you gave to me, a first-time author.

To those who challenged and mocked me, refused to be allies, and discounted me, I say thank you. At the time I couldn't understand, but you helped propel me to a place I wasn't aware I could go. Those days brought out the best in me. I no longer see you as the enemy but as stones along the rugged and sometimes smooth path to the next stage of my life. Again, thank you.

To all who purchase and read this book. Thank you. I honestly encourage you to Color Your Style! God has uniquely created you to be someone so special. Take your piece of the pie and shine. Come out of hiding and move out from behind the walls and the shadows of other people. Rise up because it's time to celebrate the authentic you.

No Room for You

Just imagine . . .

You have been asked to coordinate a special event for a small group of important people. The venue has been selected, the room for the evening event has swanky chandeliers that hang ever so perfectly from the ceiling, and a fireplace adorns the room, bringing about a definite ambience of romance. The conference-style table with twenty chairs arranged around it neatly has the perfect floral centerpiece directly under one of the shiny crystal light fixtures. The best china has been set with crisp white napkins, appropriate eating utensils, and place cards denoting seat assignments. You say to yourself, this is good.

The guests begin to arrive and gather in the reserved private room. As a gracious hostess, you smile and speak to every guest. As you mingle, one of the members of the planning team asks an interesting question: "Where are you going to sit?"

You think to yourself, what kind of question is this and why are you asking it? Well, of course I plan to sit at the table. Don't you see there is a place card with my name at the end of the table, which allows easy access to dismiss myself if needed?

As you are slowly returning from the brain spin, you respectfully answer, "I planned to sit at the table." You notice the strange, awkward look on their face—you know, the one that sets the tone for more to come. They begin to advise you that during the meeting from which they were dismissed to prepare for the guests, one of the senior managers asked where you were going to sit. Okay, now your mind is really spiraling out of control. They continue to state that an uninvited guest had arrived and needed a seat at the table. Now you know this was a futile attempt to try and sugar coat the final decision, which had been made prior to knowing of an uninvited guest. A decision made from ego and dislike for you.

What? Your thoughts go into overload, and you try to sort out what is really happening. Did anyone ask others on the team to volunteer their seats? Why was I singled out to forfeit my seat? Was there a vote or consensus, and if so, am I able to cast my vote? Who initiated this foolishness? Have I been double-crossed? All my efforts and hard work coordinating this event, and there is no room at the table for me? Your heart begins to pump faster as the adrenaline builds to the point that you could explode. Boom!

Your creative juices begin to flow as you think outside the box, searching for options—Plan A, B, or even C. You ask yourself, did they put in any effort to fix this dilemma? Or ask my opinion about some alternatives? They could have requested an additional place setting or added an extension to the table.

So where does that leave me? Is there no room for me?

Okay, I know you are saying, well an uninvited guest arrived, and isn't the dinner for important customers? So, what's so wrong with giving up your seat? Well, let's look at what is so wrong.

After reading this story, how do you really feel? Probably confused, angry, rejected, unappreciated, denied, belittled, and most of all embarrassed. You're the only one of cultural color in the room and the very one asked to give up their seat. Are you surprised? Of course not. It's nothing new for you or your ancestors to be considered the least in the room. Your title did not constitute a place for you at the table—or did it?

Please understand that this is not a fictional story; it happened to me. One of my job responsibilities was event planning. I was asked to coordinate the entire event, locate a facility, reserve sleeping accommodations, ensure the meeting room would present a professional image, select meals, schedule a cocktail hour, etc. So, to be excluded from the room that had adequate space to seat one more in lieu of an uninvited guest was not necessary. However, you never know what is being discussed behind closed doors. There was an enemy determined to keep me from the table, treating me like the help. There's nothing wrong with being the help if you are aware of it initially. But to be blindsided at the crucial hour when everyone has arrived and your name has been placed at the table, seeing it removed because the consensus is to keep you from the table, has an impact on the heart and mind.

After I composed myself, I asked the Lord for His help to get through this evening. I will be honest: I was not in that place of agreeing that all things work together for good, but eventually, after the event had successfully concluded, I was able to see the good in what had transpired.

I replaced the hat of hurt with my professional hat and proceeded to update the hotel staff on the new changes. I smiled and continued to mingle and greet the guests even though my heart had just taken a painful stabbing. It takes a lot of courage to continue to press forward despite how you are feeling. But courage is what it took, as well as a made-up mind that nothing and no one was going to steal my joy that evening. I was on an assignment, and I was determined to fulfill it.

The overwhelming kindness of the hotel staff rallying around me was awesome. It was like friends coming together for an evening of catching up and sharing. A private table was set up and my food and drink order taken, along with ongoing updates on the event I was coordinating in the adjacent room. The evening of coordinating shifted and I became the uninvited yet important guest. Happy, joyful laughter filled the area in a place that was meant to hurt me and downgrade me. You see, what the others set out to exclude, God stepped in and worked out for my good. What a great evening this turned out to be. I met new friends and took home delicious leftovers for the next day's dining pleasure. Who received the victory out of this? I did. A table was prepared for me in the presence of my enemies, and my cup did run over.

So, at the end of the evening, I chose to Color My Style and not allow this awkward position to control or overtake my emotions. I elected not to show up for this battle. We have the right to pick and choose which battles are worth our undivided attention. But never forget: whatever battle you find yourself in or facing, the overall battle belongs to the Lord! He will fight for you.

Table of Contents

The Intro

As you embark on your new journey of where life will lead you, I invite you to get on board and join me as we take a virtual expedition and discover exclusive experiences and cultural differences, uncover talents and skills, and ultimately understand the importance of stability and values in the career environment and in life in general. I want to show you how all these parts of your life relate to colors.

Upon disembarkation from this journey, you will be able to associate colors with where you are in life. Life is a journey and there are highs and lows that we move in and out of as if we were in a corn maze. Imagine a field of rich, bright yellow produce attached to tall, green stalks, ready for picking. In the same field are dry, brittle brown stalks with no life and produce lying on the ground that seems to be of no use. But don't be fooled—both have a usefulness to meet needs and, in some cases, demand. As we continue through the maze from path to path, we gaze upward at bright blue skies with white clouds appearing as oversized cotton balls, suspended in air as we reach the exit from where life has us.

But as you will experience, the story doesn't necessarily have to end due to a season of life and the path we're traveling. Some seasons seem to go on and on and can literally be overwhelming and exhausting. At times they are so draining that you wonder if you can face another day. And yet, at other times life feels free, like blowing leaves lifting and twirling on a windy day. But the hope we have is just beyond the current season because another one is ready to come alive and we can start anew!

So, let's lean into the colors of life that are all around us. See them for what they can bring into your life. Combine them and create something new and beautiful. One color can never reveal the whole story. And believe me, you and I have a story to tell.

However, for the purpose of our journey, we will spotlight the following colors: white (innocent), green (peaceful), red (energetic), blue (calm), orange (spicy), black (mysterious), and purple (royal).

Are you ready? Come on, get on board, have your tickets available—let's explore and learn how to Color Your Style! Don't you just love traveling? There's a big world waiting for us to discover.

CHAPTER 1

Cannot Tell It All – My Story

I grew up in a home with two wonderful, dedicated, hardworking parents who believed the only way to obtain your life's goals, desires, and needs was through steady employment. They taught my sister and me by being living examples and mentors. We had no pretext for the values and reality of being employed or committed to the job we would be hired to perform.

For example, I clearly remember one harsh Iowa winter with below zero temperatures in which my father's vehicle would not start. It was early in the morning, around 5:30 a.m., and I recall him going to the back porch to get his bicycle. I thought to myself, what is dad doing? So, I arose from my bed and trekked down the long staircase to humbly ask if he was going to ride the bike to work. With some fear and a love for my father, I asked, "Are you going to be okay? Why don't you use mom's car?"

But being the gracious gentleman, father, and husband that he was, combined with the unselfish love he had for my mother, he did not want her to be late arriving to her place of employment. If he pursued this, it would place both of them in a difficult position and possibly leave a blemish on their excellent attendance records. These two people were strong, committed believers in being on time and in attendance.

So instead he decided to take the hit for the team in lieu of risking them both ending up with tarnished attendance and on-time records. You must understand that a good attendance record was important because it exemplified the character of a person. It showed dedication, commitment, and, most of all, gratitude to the God who permitted the blessing. I watched him bundle up, guide the bike down the icy cement stairs, and adjust himself as he placed one leg over the middle bar of the bike, secured his lunch in the front basket, and proceeded to ride on the snow-covered sidewalks toward his destination. The trip took him over the Mississippi River to the Illinois side of the Quad Cities.

I of course went back to bed, but that day left an indelible indention in my heart and mind. Who was this man we called dad who loved us so much that he was willing to use any means of transportation to ensure he would not miss a day of work or jeopardize the final payout on his weekly check?

Who does that? I'll tell you who it is: a man or a woman who is determined not to allow life circumstances to stand in their way, but to press toward and pursue the mark of their calling.

Well, that is the type of illustration and demonstration that existed in our family on an ongoing basis.

You see, we were also taught to be in attendance and on time, whether it was school or a job. To this day, I can testify it was rare for my sister and me to allow weather or illness to deter us from the company that had hired us and entrusted us to perform a specific duty.

We often reflect and laugh at the words that were spoken over our lives daily even before we entered the work environment. The importance of school was impressed on us, and our parents did not allow us to use pitiful, inadequate excuses to avoid the institution of education, which they understood would be one of the many vehicles molding our future.

Let me tell you about my one and only sister, May, whom I love dearly. During her elementary school years, she was good at trying to avoid school. If she felt like today was not a good day to be in school, she could instantly become ill and be sent to the school nurse, who would coddle her with an apple or snack and allow her to lie down on one of those twin-size steel army cots covered with a gray wool blanket. One day when she was dealing with my sister's antics of not feeling well, the nurse decided to contact our mother at her place of employment. Now, don't forget what I explained earlier about the examples we were shown of being a good, moral employee and student. Mom politely listened and then asked the nurse to put my sister on the phone. You can only imagine what was said during that one-on-one conversation. However, Mom lovingly proceeded to give May an uncompromising chastisement and demanded she return to class. And before she hung up the phone, the hot warning was given: "Don't let me receive another phone call if you are not really sick. Now get back to class."

Today, as adults, thinking of this situation brings us to tears with laughter. We really had to be seriously ill in order to miss any days from school. I am still not sure why we thought we could outsmart our parents. They were young and innocent at one time, and they tried the same tricks with their parents and failed. But you can't blame us for trying, right?

Our parents were strong-minded and strong-willed, determined to see us receive a good education and be triumphant in life. Life did not always hand them a joyride on their road to success.

They both grew up in large families with low income. In my father's case, he was mandated to leave school in the sixth grade to help care for the farm and family. I asked him how he had felt about being pulled from school and friends, and his reply was that he'd had to do what was required of him. Yet my father's extraction from school at a young age did not deter him from moving forward with a sixth-grade education and obtaining a full-time factory job as an assembler with a prestigious company known for manufacturing farm equipment. He made a decent salary and was able to provide for his family. We lived a good middle-class life and our needs and wants were taken care of.

We were not denied the basics of food, clothing, and shelter or some simple desires in life. Our Christmas holidays were filled with joy and laughter as we assembled the silver tinsel tree, inserting its branches into the wooden pole with holes and then adorning it with colorful bulbs—some with liquid inside that added a special touch.

There were absolutely no disparities or biased treatment from our parents. They made sure we were treated equally and there was no room for thinking their love extended to one more than the other. Our gifts were pretty much the same with one exception: the color. So now you see how color played an important role in my life even as a young child. They ensured the gift's color denoted who it rightfully belonged to. So, if my pink record player broke, I could not go and claim my sister's player or vice versa. During these times of gift-giving, color conveyed ownership.

We were blessed that our parents allowed us to invite friends on vacation and host overnight stay-overs. To this day, the friends that my sister grew up with still talk about the love extended beyond our family to touch their families. Clothes and toys that were not being used were donated not only our friends but to total strangers. No selfishness or greed was allowed with the blessings that God bestowed upon us. In my adult life, it reminds me of the Bible scripture in Luke 6:38 (KJV): *"Give, and it shall be given to you; good measure, pressed down, and shaken together, and running over."* We were not rich, but we shared what we had. And God continually blessed and increased what we had as we imparted it to others.

An example is the occasional Sunday fish fries that brought our families together. My father would cook the catch of the weekend along with johnny cakes, coleslaw, and Louisiana hot sauce for a table of hungry, eager relatives and friends who were ready to dine sufficiently. The colorful discussions around the meal, along with old stories, made Sundays a great gathering time. All of this was a part of my parents giving back and sharing their good fortune.

There are so many stories and examples I could tell you about my parents' joy in giving back. You know, sometimes people will give and then complain. I have never seen or experienced this type of behavior from my parents. They have always extended hope with a smile, ready to help the next individual in need.

Our father, Mayfield, retired after a total of twenty-eight years of service with a respectable pension and enough Social Security stored up to live a modest lifestyle. It is now so clear to me that he did not allow the obstacle of his life circumstance as a youngster removed from elementary school to hinder him from pursuing a solid career to take care of his family. I never heard my father grumble or blame anyone for his upbringing. He did not allow the past to determine his future.

He could have easily used this as an excuse to wiggle out of his head-of-household responsibilities. Yet he embraced them and found areas to be thankful for. Self-determination was written all over his life, and he passed it to his two daughters. He and Mom constantly reinforced the importance of pursuing our dreams with the understanding that we had their support 100 percent. We lost him in January 2020, but the lessons he instilled in us still live on within us, lessons like "If you want respect, give respect" and "Treat others as you want to be treated." I once heard someone say, "Well, maybe they don't want to be treated as I want to be treated." My answer to this comment is think of what you are giving out and make sure you can handle having it returned to you.

Ms. Earnestine, our mother, the oldest of twelve siblings, completed high school and as a married adult attended an evening trade school to obtain her certification in manufacturing piecework. After completing the night courses, she landed a full-time job with a company that manufactured pumps for a variety of customers. She eventually retired from this company after a total of thirty-three years of service.

However, she began her career as a young woman who worked in her high school cafeteria, and because of this her brothers and sisters were guaranteed a free hot meal. She assisted in a beauty shop, washing clients' hair, in which the owner led her to a rewarding role in modeling. She remained a stay-at-home mom until my younger sister entered kindergarten and I was in the second grade.

Please do not misunderstand the life of my mother. She was like a sleeping giant. There were no issues or concerns from her until you climbed that beanstalk and woke her out of her sleep. You may be thinking, with all this talk about a career, did she ever have obstacles to tunnel through or have to find a path around naysayers? The answer is yes. It was not strange to overhear my parents talking about their career strategy when confronted with a manager who offended them or was not functioning honestly or equally.

I can recall a time when a manager was making an obvious conscious difference in how each employee on his team was treated. My mother confronted the supervisor, then took it to HR, and when no resolution was clear, she went directly to the top, the president. Yes, you read that right: the president of the company. She drafted a letter describing the actions of the supervisor and the non-response from HR. Do you know that president showed up to the facility unannounced and, to everyone's surprise, dealt with the leadership team?

When she tells the story, first you value the president of the company. He listened to an employee's distresses, then concocted the decision to visit unannounced, which showcased his stand for the culture he expected from the company and its leadership. This audacious move ensured that, moving forward, all employees would be treated with respect and dignity for the job they were performing.

Do you agree we need more senior, middle, and first-level managers to demonstrate this type of behavior? If we had more leaders who exhibited such allyship with their staff, I believe companies would be better and staff would be happier. Happy people, appreciated people, will go the extra mile to ensure the success of their place of employment.

Remember the song "If You're Happy and You Know It"? The words simply say:

If you're happy and you know it

Then your face will surely show it

If you're happy and you know it

Clap your hands.

When you're happy and you feel your best, it does something to you. You move differently, work smarter, and smile more. There's a good feeling on the inside that shows up on the outside, and other people see it as well. You'll notice them smiling back at you because you are glowing with confidence.

Let's get back to the story.

Now, the tenacity of my mother and her courage to take steps toward a resolution that would guarantee justice for all deserves an award. You see, it only takes one person to make a difference in any situation. On that day, Mrs. Earnestine Hall's valor Colored Her Style.

She made an impact that inundated the company with equal treatment for everyone and held all involved accountable. She was a force not to be messed with, but the only way she could be this effective was through the experience she gained during her previous working history.

She gained the respect of the company's senior management due to her dedication, hard work, great attendance, and total commitment to the company. Never think no one is paying attention to you or your efforts. I am reminded of a senior neighbor who once told me, "Never think no one sees you or what you are doing—they may not know you, but someone is always looking."

There is absolutely no way what you do goes unnoticed. It may not be senior management, a school principal, a counselor, a pastor, etc., but your effort and work will undoubtedly touch a coworker or someone you have never met.

From our parents, we learned we must stand for what is right. Taking a stand could cause you to lose your job or set the new tone for treating others with the respect they deserve. The choice is yours—it's up to you.

After retirement, my mother fulfilled several items on her bucket list, one of which was to travel the world. I can still hear the excitement in her voice as she phoned my sister and me and began to reveal her life desires. Finally, after working for thirty-three years, she was free to pursue her dreams with no binding ties. Here was our first opportunity to experience the color style of our mother and her dreams.

The next directive from her was "Girls, let's see the world!" And I'm telling you that is just what we did. We created a plan of action for our travel. Our first international trip was mom's choice: London and Paris, here we come! These were two cities filled with love, life, and, most importantly, color. And every year after that initial trip, we rotated who would select our next destination with the caveat that the other two travelers could not complain or try to sway the selector's final vacation destination. This method uncovered the colors of each of us. The choice each year was the selector's bucket list dream, and we would join without hesitation. I was promoted to official travel agent, so I handled all the arrangements through my personal travel agent and maintained the travel documents.

We began as inexperienced international travelers and soon become three of the most experienced travelers—a mother and her two daughters. People in every country were impressed at the fact that a mother and her daughters had such a close relationship in which they could travel the world with no issues or arguments, only true love and respect for each other. It was apparent that our color styles meshed well together. My mother's friends and some of ours envied our relationship and would say, "I wish I could travel and have the type of union you have."

It is no secret that due to the seeds of life placed in us by our parents, my sister and I were employed with stable, strong companies and our mother retired with a good income. We had no financial challenges in discovering this great big world. Allow to me to say we were blessed and highly favored.

So, it became apparent to my sister and me that the past sermons preached worked for our good. If we did not have the examples of our parents, dedicated and committed employees who worked with integrity, we would lack the wisdom and funds to afford us the opportunities to experience some of the best this earth offers. We took on the world and Colored Our Style!

You know, after the passing of our mother, my sister and I continued down the path of seeing the world. And as we sit on each airplane, we reminisce and say, "Mom would like this place and have a big, beautiful smile on her face." She loved to travel, especially with her girls. She will never be forgotten.

Today I hold on tight to my wonderful memories of helping my mother fulfill her dreams of seeing the big, beautiful world. We missed one major place on her list and that was Australia. But one day I vow to visit Australia in her honor. We love and miss you, Ms. Earnestine—our mother.

Looking back at the passing of our parents, we are thankful for their love and commitment to us, a commitment that drove us to pursue the finer things in life and to take this work concept to another level. My sister, with thirty years of employment, retired at the sweet age of fifty-five years old as a field engineer with a master's degree. I'm a director of facilities with twenty-seven years of employment and a bachelor of science degree. These are career accomplishments to be proud of, and we know our parents would be equally thrilled.

Their vision for us came to fulfillment. We never assisted with the gray hairs on their heads or with problems or issues, but embraced them as role models and took the ride to sweet freedom. Freedom to choose where you want to go in life. Freedom to pursue the education of your choice and move to the next level. Freedom to make the final decision as to how long you want to dwell in a company, relationship, etc. Sweet freedom.

As you move through the journey of being an employee or owner of your own business, if you have not proven yourself to be a true asset to the company, then when situations appear, it will be difficult to fight with no ammunition or troops on your side. A good soldier needs to always be ready.

So, I admonish you to build up your reputation, be honest, be committed, show up, and be counted as a worthy employee who will always outshine those who try to belittle your worth, defame you, put you down, or put their foot on your neck. In other words, you need a leg to stand on so that if or when there is a bad circumstance, you can defend your cause.

Never forget, as I stated earlier, there is always someone looking at your lifestyle and watching how you handle life's situations. Please don't misunderstand me. No, we don't exist for others, but don't be fooled—others are looking. We are living examples; our lives are testimonies whether we choose for them to be or not. So, Color Your Style with care and discernment.

Journey Pause:

Have you ever viewed your life as a living example? Well, whether you believe it or not, your life and my life can and will affect others. The expectation for you and me is that it affects others in a positive manner.

Crossroad Enlightenment:

"Let your light so shine before men, that they may see your good works, and glorify your Father which is in heaven" (Matthew 5:16, KJV).

Color – White

(Innocence, Goodness, Cleanness, Peace)

CHAPTER 2

The Journey Begins

Arise to the brightness of **white** as the sun shines and through your windows, clean, innocent, and crisp without flaws. It's a new day!

....

I have always been intrigued and awed at the presence of color. Color can transform a room that was once gray and drab into a beautiful paradise for lovers, a chaotic space into one of serenity and peace, a playroom into a rainbow with harmony of color that invites children to laugh and smile.

Color can illuminate a person who typically shies away from being noticed like a beautiful bouquet of flowers blooming with life.

I love the warm hues of earth tones in my home with clean, opulent white walls. However, when it comes to my wardrobe, I tend to lean toward bright and bold shades of fabrics.

Color is an instant mood changer and can shift a cloudy attitude to a sunny one that lingers throughout the day. Most of us can recall a time when what we wore caused others to react. Sometimes they react out of surprise that you dared to wear that color and sometimes because of the new glow that has you beaming like the early morning sun as it penetrates through the window. You came alive!

I can't recall the number of times I have been complimented on my wardrobe selection that included bold colors. Dressing is a satisfying yet simple task that brightens not only your day but someone else's as well. I've had many people ask, "Isn't that a lot of work to go through each day?"

I reply, "Putting together this outfit was no different from when you chose what you are wearing now. Effort is not the hard part—it's the desire to be your best in whatever Colors Your Style."

It's interesting that we decorate our homes, the dwelling we call our sanctuary, our retreat of protection, with various colors of furniture, walls, and accessories that showcase our personalities and style, yet find ourselves running from the very thing that bring happiness: color.

Why can't we live together—people of color, all colors, all nationalities, all cultures, all mixtures—and unite strong under God's great heavens? Instead of running from each other, avoiding one-on-one interaction, we need to open the doors to get to know each other. Don't you know that when I get to know you, it's as if our unique colors dance together in harmony? Would you like to dance?

God created the heavens and the earth in six days full of color (see Genesis 1). The earth was without form and void. Darkness was upon the deep, and He moved upon the face of the waters. He divided the light from the dark, made the firmament, and divided the waters under the firmament from the waters above it. He called the firmament heaven. He gathered the waters under heaven into one place and dry land appeared, called earth. God told the earth to bring forth grass, herb yielding seed, and fruit trees yielding fruit. He commanded light to appear in the firmament of the heavens to divide day and night and the signs of the seasons.

He made two great lights, the greater to rule the day and the lesser to rule the night. Both lights beam with the brightness of the color white. The greater, which is the sun, shines as a bright light bulb lighting up the skies, providing light to a dark room called earth. The lesser light, the moon, with its off-white subtleness, brings light to a dark sky and joining twinkling lights that appear to the eye like white dots dancing in the sky. The lesser light is different from the light that rules the day, but both have their own purpose and uniqueness that impart illumination to the world. However, can you imagine where we would be without these two great lights? It is sure that we would see only in black, never experiencing the magnificence of color—color that activates the darkness, ushering in energy and life.

Next, He told the waters to bring forth abundant fowl that fly and created great whales and every living creature that moves, beasts of the earth and everything that creeps on the earth.

"Then God said, Let us make man in our image, after our likeness: and let them have dominion over the fish of the sea, over the fowl of the air, and over the cattle, and over all the earth, and over every creeping thing" (Genesis 1:26). God saw everything He had made, and behold, it was exceptionally good, full of awesome colors.

As you read the first chapter of Genesis, the creation of the world comes alive. You can see the colors coming into play as God created. Can you see the heavens and the bright blue skies with clouds perfectly positioned to decorate them, the sun shining and bringing forth a warmth to the skin, and the whales, dark and gray as they play and swim in large turquoise blue pools called the seas and oceans?

See the cattle, brown and taupe and speckled with white as they graze on green, luscious, grassy hills? Trees filled with an abundance of fruit? Colors coming alive?

Whether it is the fearlessness of red, the spicy touch of orange, the royalty of purple, the freshness of green, the sophistication of black and white, or the cool calm of blue, all hues have their special place within our everyday lives.

God knew color would be needed to separate, distinguish, coordinate, unify, and brighten our days here on Earth. However, color was not meant to divide as it is portrayed today, with one color or race thinking and believing they are better than another. In fact, we all are created equal and precious in God's sight. Whose sight or whose report will we believe—mankind's or God's? How can one color rule the world in all its glory? How can one color take preeminence above another? Can you imagine God creating this world with one primary color? How drab, how dreary, how uncreative, how unexciting—just humdrum. But it's not so. Our God is a God of color! But, thanks be to God, we know in fact He is a God of excitement, color, imagination, creativity, originality, innovation, and more. We all belong here because God makes no mistakes! So why can't we live in this big world called Earth together, sharing, loving, and enjoying the creations of our Creator? Why live beneath your privilege when God has granted life with color?

Whatever color palette lightens up your day or puts a smile on your face reflects and ascribes to the uniqueness in you the character that can only be performed by you and enthused by you.

Psalms 139:14 (KJV) states, *"I will praise thee; for I am fearfully and wonderfully made: marvelous are they works; and that my soul knoweth right well."* God, the Greatest and Chief Architect, had a design for you and me from the beginning. The Master Builder had the master plan with minute details positioning us where He desired to achieve His purpose and calling in our lives. It is no mistake that you are who you are. The way you look, act, feel, and respond to life with its never-ending circumstances are all part of His architectural design plan for you.

Have you ever wondered why you handle a situation differently from your spouse, siblings, or friends? Well, it's all a part of the master plan weaved into your life, knitted and constructed to withstand the test of time.

For example, let's say you study long hours and days for an important test that will catapult you to the next level. When the examination day finally arrives, you are confident you will pass because you prayed, dedicated time to study, and gained assurance that you understand the subject matter. However, after taking the exam, you are informed you failed.

What just happened? You are devasted, disappointed, and so confused. Someone should score the test again. How can this be? you ask yourself.

Now the question is, how would you handle this situation based on your special design features? For some, it would be over and they would move on. However, you were designed differently. You see a bigger picture, you are not defeated, and you go back to the drawing board. You know why? I'll tell you why: because your Chief Architect created you with determination and self-will to achieve what you're trying to accomplish. You have been given a never-give-up mindset.

An architect, according to Merriam-Webster.com Dictionary, is a person who designs buildings and, in many cases, also supervises their construction. It's a person who is responsible for inventing or realizing a particular ideas or project.

Oh yes, we have a purpose in this life, and it would behoove us to seek God to understand exactly what it is. He has made you special, and no one can duplicate you or take what has been instilled in you. The fake knockoff will try to imitate you, but their tactics will be uncovered and revealed for all to see. What is in you will last a lifetime. As you mature, not just in age but in life experience, your color style may change, but it remains uniquely you. Even though you didn't purchase it or work for it, you own it, so embrace it. Did you know each of us is an original?

Let's look at Galatians 5:25–26 (MSG): *"Since this is the kind of life we have chosen, the life of the Spirit, let us make sure that we do not just hold it as an idea in our heads or a sentiment in our hearts, but work out its implications in every detail of our lives. That means we will not compare ourselves with each other as if one of us were better and another worse. We have far more interesting things to do with our lives. Each of us is an original."*

Have you ever visited an art gallery? I love visiting art galleries and museums. The buildings are quiet and so still, allowing the visitors to take in what is being presented. The atmosphere devotes itself to giving you an unexpected experience. Each exhibit or painting is an original telling a story through the eyes of the designer, the artist. I like seeing how the imagination of the artist comes alive with colors dancing together on the canvas. Sunsets in bright orange fade away, making room for evening. The whitecaps of the blue seas point upward in a raging storm. As you stand and gaze at the paintings with their colors ever so bold or sometimes muted, you can almost experience the pull of the artist coming from the depths of their heart and imagination to create this one-of-a-kind original filled with love and passion—a wonderful work of art.

God has sanctioned four seasons within a year, and each one bears a new set of colors. Spring begins the budding of something new, summer enters and nourishes spring's precursor, then fall removes what summer has fulfilled and prepares for winter to shield and hibernate what spring will bring forth once again. And the cycle of seasons repeats itself. In cycles of seasons or cycles of life, we experience the same rotation patterns.

As stated in Ecclesiastes 3:1–2 (KJV), *"To everything there is a season, and a time to every purpose under the heaven. A time to be born, and a time to die; a time to plant, and a time to pluck up that which is planted; a time to kill, and a time to heal; a time to break down, and a time to build up; a time to weep, and a time to laugh; a time to mourn, and a time to dance; a time to cast away stones, and a time to gather stones together; a time to embrace, and a time to refrain from embracing; a time to get, and a time to lose; a time to keep, and a time to cast away; a time to rend, and a time to sew; a time to keep silence, and a time to speak; a time to love, and a time to hate; a time of war, and a time of peace."*

There are prosperous seasons of life that bring life, joy, and happiness. These are the colorful times. But sometimes the next season seems to transport you to another world filled with sadness, hard times of struggling surrounded by endless gray days and even death. And yet these are also colorful times. It is called life, and there are no warning signs to prepare you for what is about to come. There is no detailed, step-by-step procedural manual for expecting the season we will experience at any given time or managing the process when it arrives.

Despite the lack of a manual, it is wise to be cognizant of our seasons. This is not an easy task because we can become consumed by a troubled season's effect on our life.

We can get stuck in a color or season and allow gray days to lead versus clear, bright blue, sunshiny days. We must fight back to allow growth, opportunities, and, most of all, victory—victory in the heart and the mind.

There is a powerful scripture, Philippians 4:8–9 (MSG): *"Summing it all up, friends, I'd say you'll do best by filling your minds and meditating on things true, noble, reputable, authentic, compelling, gracious—the best, not the worst; the beautiful, not the ugly; things to praise, not things to curse. Put into practice what you learned from me, what you heard and saw and realized. Do that, and God, who makes everything work together, will work you into his most excellent harmonies."*

You and I can obtain the victory in our seasonal encounters, whether they are pleasant or unpleasant. Speak to yourself and be determined to get up, fight back, take charge, and move toward a new season and color. Now take control and Color Your Style.

How can we run from color and think the world is just some one-size-fits-all? We live in a world of color—accept it. Make up your mind that it will not change, it is permanent. It's like a magic marker. Use it on the wrong material, like a whiteboard, and you won't be able to remove it. It's been strategically projected in the design. Color is here to stay. It was affirmed and established before the heavens and earth were formed.

We share color within our cultural differences. Brighter hues are generally associated with indigenous cultures, while earthy tones, muted with minimal vibrant colors, are seen in other cultures. But one thing that is clear and mutual is color. Color is what makes the world unique and special. It's a sister to the colorful seasons of life.

Just imagine: before there was a world or you and me, God declared that color would rule and be an important part of our everyday lives. Can you imagine a world without color?

We, as humans, must stop seeing each other as opposites based on the colors in which we were created—equal and yet so unique. Color, color, oh, how beautiful you are, and what joy you bring to this world! We can have harmony together as we share this big universal space created by God, surrounded and endowed with color.

As we grow together, life becomes so rich and vibrant. Our styles, talents, and skills mesh into this wonderful combination, almost like a one-of-a-kind dessert. It's been mixed by the hand of the highest qualified chef, unifying all its ingredients, and the final product is you and me.

If creation can come together and allow room for seasons to usher in their individual contributions to the world, why is it so challenging for mankind, you and me, to allow room for our brothers and sisters to contribute to this habitation we call home? We have all been built into God's plan whether you believe it or not. Each of us has been given a plan of promise to fulfill.

So be brave, announce yourself without saying a word to a waiting world. Ready or not, here I come—Color My Style!

Journey Pause:

In our first stop, we've discovered the color white, which references a fresh start, a new page, innocence, and peace. Remember, you are an original. The Master Builder, the Chief Architect, has equipped you with everything you need to fulfill your purpose. Now look at yourself in the mirror and say, "I am an original."

Crossroad Enlightenment: Peaceful

"If it is possible, as far as it depends on you, live at peace with everyone" (Romans 12:18, NIV).

"Don't hit back; discover beauty in everyone. If you've got it in you, get along with everybody. Don't insist on getting even; that's not for you to do. 'I'll do the judging,' says God. 'I'll take care of it'" (Romans 12:17–19, MSG).

Note: At the end of this chapter, we begin the building process with the colors. We use an octagon shape in the color of white.

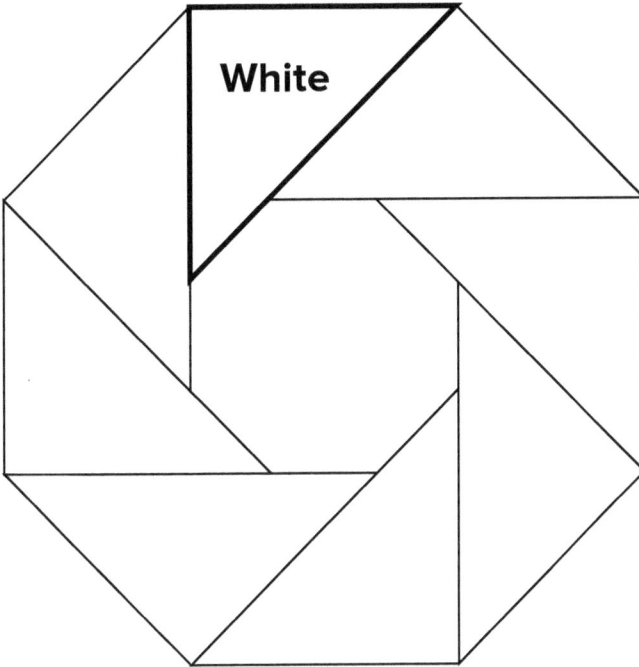

White

Color – Green

(Fresh, Organic, Loyal, Aware, Secure, Peaceful)

C H A P T E R 3

Press Toward The Mark

Look to the meadows painted in the peaceful color **green.** Come lie down in green pastures. He'll lead you beside still waters and send you in the right direction (Psalm 23).

....

As we begin making mature decisions and trying to figure out our path, we (my sister and I) discovered our education was good and it opened the door for us to be employed by well-known corporations that people dreamed of working for. We were blessed and favored, but really did not understand just how fortunate we were. Honestly, we were just grateful to have a good job as our parents had instructed and mentored us to.

Everything you will experience in life is launched from a foundation. Whether these experiences are good or bad, we do not just become or arrive, but something is placed and rooted, tested and established, during our experiences. Then it is poured calmly to secure a lasting, solid footing.

Where did you learn your moral values or integrity that at times seem to speak in a small, still voice, sometimes chastising and other times congratulating? It started from the fundamental, foundational truths that you observed or were taught. Most of us began gathering these foundational truths from our parents or grandparents in a process known as good old home training. Or maybe you were adopted by some great people, such as a schoolteacher or counselor who instilled in you what they learned from their past experiences, molding you to face what was ahead on this path of life.

Whatever the method or the person who instilled great wisdom, in most cases that wisdom will never be forgotten. When you look back over your life, it's as if you're looking in the rearview mirror, giving thanks or reminiscing in joy at the techniques they used to drive the message home.

The way you build your career, business, and life is generally based on your foundation. No building can stand without a proper foundation that has been dug deep to withstand winds, pressures, earthquakes, and other stress. It takes a firm foundation to maintain a life that is grounded and secure, a firm foundation that will not shift with every whim life brings. However, sometimes life brings a force that may not crumble or destroy the foundation, but leaves a crack of remembrance. Remember, though, a crack can be repaired with the proper tools, sustaining the structure for years to come. This sustaining ability can only occur based on the architectural design created by the Designer of your life.

During my last year of high school, I was able to participate as an off-site co-op student with one of the top manufacturing employers in my hometown. Do you see a pattern here? If you remember, in an earlier chapter I told you both of my parents worked manufacturing jobs. However, I was able to participate because I completed all the required classes for graduation except one. So, I had time to begin launching a new adventure to carry me toward adulthood and secure my future. I was grateful to be given the opportunity to work outside the school campus.

I knew I wasn't like my classmates early in my life. What was important to me at that time was totally different from what mattered to those I sat with in the classroom. Honestly, I didn't participate in the activities that my fellow classmates found important.

At the age of seventeen, I was making a salary that was notable and yet overwhelming to someone in my age group. One day I had a serious conversation with my mother about this new means of financial overflow. My question was "I have so much money, I don't know what to do with it. What should I do?" As a mother of great wisdom, she advised me that the best move was to begin saving. Well, as you can see from the response, this was another opportunity to instill yet another learning moment to move me through life. Don't spend everything that you acquire, but always put something away for a rainy day. Mom was a big advocate for saving, and we heard her thoughts, observed her, and respected her as a great role model. As a matter of fact, we had a Christmas Club savings account at an early age to inspire and train us in the importance of saving. So, when it was time to purchase holiday gifts, we had the means to accomplish this. I can remember the feeling of achievement and yet thankfulness for the nudge to save, which allowed us to bless someone else.

The new parent sermon text now is "work, save, and give." I am a huge fan of this philosophy, and it is an integral part of my life today. What we obtain in life is only partially ours. We are blessed to bless someone else. Don't get me wrong—you are not required to give all your good fortune away, but don't despise humble beginnings. If you can help jump-start someone else, do it. We all had the support of someone to begin at this unforgettable place in life. So, transfer the good values of sharing and giving to the next generation. Don't hold it all for yourself. What joy is there in that kind of mindset? Remember, it's not all about monetary sharing. It reaches way beyond that—it can be returned in giving your time, taking part in outreach initiatives, and other contributions.

Let's stop listening to the negative chatter that discourages us from helping our neighbor. A neighbor is not necessarily the person next door to where you reside, but everyone is our neighbor. If you see a need and have the means to assist, why not reach out and touch someone's life? You could be the answer to make their world a better place.

As this chapter concludes, we have gained the importance of education, graduating, landing a secure job, and receiving wisdom about the value of both saving what you have earned and sharing it.

Now I present part 2 of inspiring words to live by from my parents: "I'm not always going to be in a place to bail you out." Yes, you read that right. What Mom was telling us is that she and Dad, as our parents, were not always going to be around or able to bail us out of life's challenges. The same is true of your parents or caregivers. However, if you prepare yourself in one or more areas—education, work, saving, and giving—there is a strong possibility that one of those values could pull you out of a serious situation later. So, if we have these values to fall back on, it could alleviate some of the hardship that could be placed on us.

In an earlier paragraph, I spoke about sharing and giving back to our neighbor. Who knows? They may be the ones who will give to you in your time of need. We don't give to receive; we give to bless and be a blessing.

You are probably saying to yourself, wow, your parents were full of advice and insight. Yes, that is correct, and I am sure if you look back on your life, you will see some of the same characteristics from your parents or mentors.

You see, life is life, and we are all going through it whether we want to or not. It stares at you constantly like a predator waiting for its turn. It can creep up on you, or you can stand strong, waiting to punch back. There is no getting around it, and why would you want to? The experiences will forever be etched in your heart and mind. And what is etched will not be forgotten. At times you will wear it like a beautiful pendant etched with words of strength, possibility, and encouragement. It will guide you through this sometimes tumultuous but audacious life.

I believe, therefore, that our parents, grandparents, teachers, mentors, and others we look up to have such great stories. I honestly believe we all must walk our own paths. But if you are a wise person, you can avoid a lot of heartaches, pain, and drama if you just take the time to listen and dissect some of the stories and advice that come from those who have walked the path of life and crossed over the Jordan River before you.

I call a person who fits this description a trailblazer, "a person who blazes a trail for others to follow through unsettled country or wilderness; pathfinder" (Merriam-Webster.com Dictionary). These trailblazers learned from their ancestors and found truth to pass the baton of life to the next generation.

When our time comes to pass the baton of life experiences, we must do the same to help someone along the way. We can be the missing critical piece in someone else's success. The experience may have been difficult for you, but it can help keep someone else from failing or going down the wrong path. We now become the mentor, the coach who helps them be a better person. Never think your story, whether accomplished or flawed, is yours and yours alone. Someone else will unfortunately take the same path in their life, and maybe you can provide a word of encouragement or guidance.

Are you familiar with the story of Elisha and Elijah, who were two of the most prominent prophets helping to restore Israel? In 2 Kings 2, Elisha understood that Elijah would soon pass away, and he asked to be blessed with a double portion of Elijah's spirit. Wow, can you imagine making such a bold request? A double portion of his spirit? But when you have walked, observed, gleaned, and received instructions from your mentor, I believe you can ask such a request. So, when Elijah was carried into heaven in a chariot of fire, Elisha picked up Elijah's mantle and used it to cross the Jordan on dry land. He received what he had asked for – a double portion and performed many miracles thereafter. His training now comes into full bloom. And I believe because he sat sitting and listening to wisdom from his mentor (trailblazer) helped him as he took on the journey of his life's mission.

On-the-job training is another way to move your career forward. In most businesses, educational assistance is available to help you excel in your present position and move you upward. I obtained my bachelor of science with educational assistance from my employer. Research the benefits that are available through your employer and take advantage of what is offered.

As you pursue your educational growth and obtain various degrees and certifications, all of these lead to an excellent passage in your journey as you press toward the mark that Colors Your Style. However, don't frown on modest beginnings. A well-known driving force that still brightens the eyes of most employers is experience. Experience discloses stability and dedication. It reveals who you are and how you would perform for the potential new employer. No employer wants to hire a slacker, an unmotivated individual, to work in their company. And I can only assume you do not want to have or present that type of image to any employer.

Do you think that if Elisha was an unmotivated student, his request would have been granted? I'm not sure, but what we know is that he was a studious student, adventurous and ready to learn and grow.

So, anchor yourself for the long haul and glean as much knowledge as you can while performing the job and from your trailblazer. Few opportunities in life change overnight, but in the end, if you hang in there and endure, it will prove to be a great advantage for you.

Journey Pause:

So, as we press toward the mark, our journey has rested on green. This color has rich meanings like life, energy, ambition, renewal, and new growth. It's the color of green lights. You have permission to go and do something amazing with your life, gleaning along the way from trailblazers and mentors. Combined, this permission and these resources denote relationships joined together harmoniously to transport us to the next stage. Get set and go!

Crossroad Enlightenment: Loyal

"A new commandment I give unto you, that ye love one another; as I have loved you, that ye also love one another. By this shall all men know that ye are my disciples, if ye have love one to another" (John 13:34–35, KJV).

Note: It's the end of the chapter, and we are adding green to the design. We now have white and green octagon symbols. Let's keep building.

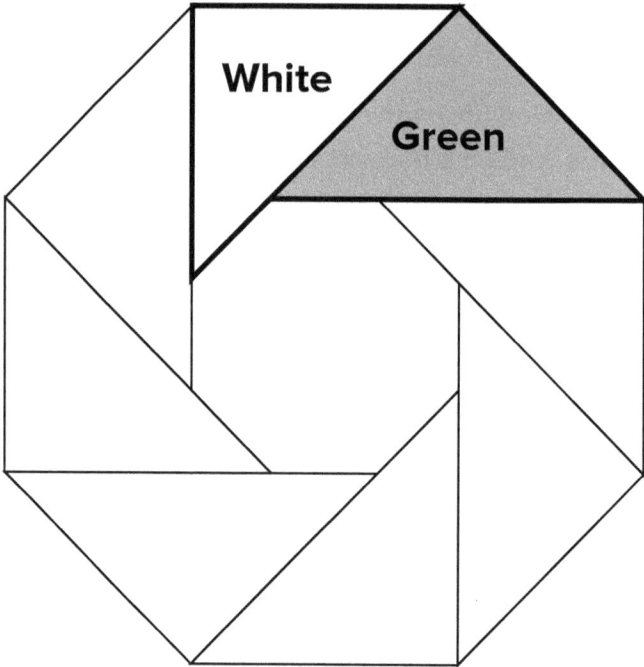

Color – Red

(Determined, Passionate, Dramatic,
Energetic, Optimistic, Brave)

C H A P T E R   4

Stumbling Blocks Along The Way

Be wise, stay alert—**red** warns us of possible danger with stop signs, stop lights, and at times life's circumstances. It tells us to proceed with caution.

....

There is no sense in thinking you can follow the path to success without having to overcome some stumbling blocks or obstacles along the way. The key is to not allow them to deter you from your goals. When you experience them along the path and understand what or who they are, you will learn how to maneuver through life. Obstacles can come in different forms, almost like a roaring lion seeking whom he may devour—sitting and waiting quietly for the next victim. However, don't let the red octagon sign with white letters stop you from chasing your goals and dreams.

Maybe you are asking whether I've conquered my obstacles. The answer to that question is twofold: yes and no. It depends on where I am in life. If the goal I was pressing toward has been reached, the obstacles have been conquered but have left an indelible mark on my life. However, any new goals or pursuits will surely bring a Goliath—big or small—trying to block progress. Anytime you are heading in a positive onward direction, there will always be stumbling blocks or obstacles to test your faith and endurance.

What is a stumbling block? According to Wikipedia at the time of writing, "a stumbling block or scandal in the Bible, or in politics (including history), is a metaphor for a behaviour attitude that leads another to sin or to destructive behaviour."

Let me tell you, I could provide plenty of examples of stumbling blocks during my lifetime that kept me on my knees, looking to my God for deliverance and guidance on the next move.

Most of the time, obstacles seem to come out of nowhere. Your life is going well and then bam, you're side-punched and sometimes knocked down in the boxing ring of life as the referee begins the countdown. The voice of the crowd, your internal voice, begins to taunt and shout: Get up! Are you going to let them get the victory? So, you gather yourself from the floor, shake yourself off, review what just happened, cry, scream, stomp your feet, and fistfight with that invisible opponent called air. You may have to take a reality check, step back, and replay the scenario to obtain a good grasp of what just occurred.

But then you must tell yourself it is not over, make up your mind to get up, and get it together because if you stay down, your opponent wins the fight. You didn't start the fight, but this time you must show up for the fight.

Remember, this is not a physical fistfight, but an internal battle of the mind. The mind can play horrible tricks on us, making us think we are losers. And if you are not careful, it can begin to cloud your judgment, which can produce low self-esteem, insecurity, or a throw-in-the-towel mentality. It can rise as insecurity in your abilities, skills, and talents. But it's not true—you know how to perform the function or duty. You were made for this, and no one can take that from you. Do not deceive or self-sabotage yourself with negative talk or thoughts. You are not defeated until you lie down, give up, and begin to meander in your own pool of humiliation or in the boxing ring of self-pity as the crowd laughs and screams, insulting your abilities. Understand there will always be individuals who are resolved that you won't succeed. So, if they're successful, you'll stop believing in the promises and plans established for your life.

But don't allow yourself to get to that point, and if you do, perform a self-diagnosis. Examine yourself and determine what your next move will be. Honestly, you may decide the fight is not worth the headache or effort and it is time to move to a new territory, a new opponent. Or you may decide it's time to get back in the ring and fight back. There comes a point in life when we cannot run from every obstacle or stumbling block. If you find yourself running, you will continue to run and never face your opposition. This does not always mean physical face-to-face encounters, but a made-up mind to keep pursuing despite the blow that knocked you down. Remember, you were born to win.

At times it may look like the situation or incident is winning in this boxing ring of life. But as you fight back, you must know and believe that victory belongs to you, and you are not punching it out alone. Heaven is cheering for you.

I'm reminded of a song:

Never alone

I don't have to worry because I'm never alone

He walks beside me all the way

He guides my footsteps every day

Never alone

Now it is time to gear up and put a mental plan of action in place, renew your strength, enter the ring again, and listen for the bell that starts the fight. Only this time, go in with your gloves and headgear on, mouth guard in (guard your speech), and hands up. Stand strong with a determined, clear mind and focus and say, "I'm in this to win. I will not be defeated. I must keep fighting for what I believe to be true. I'm made for this."

Journey Pause:

Red represents being **determined**—to pursue your goals despite the obstacles, **passionate**—about what you enjoy doing, **dramatic**—about what pushes you in life, **energetic**—to use your energy and direct it toward what matters to you, **optimistic**—confident that you can achieve the goals that have been set, and **brave**—fearless in your pursuit.

We have discovered at this Journey Pause that stumbling blocks will come our way. No one is exempt from these blocks, which appear in various forms. But when you arrive at this place along the journey, you must stop, refocus, look the obstacles in the face, make a decision to move past them, or retreat, allowing the opposition the title of conqueror.

Crossroad Enlightenment: Brave

"Yet in all these things we are more than conquerors through Him who loved us" (Romans 8:37, NKJV).

Note: It's the end of the chapter, and we are adding red to the design. We now have white, green, and red octagon symbols. Let's keep building.

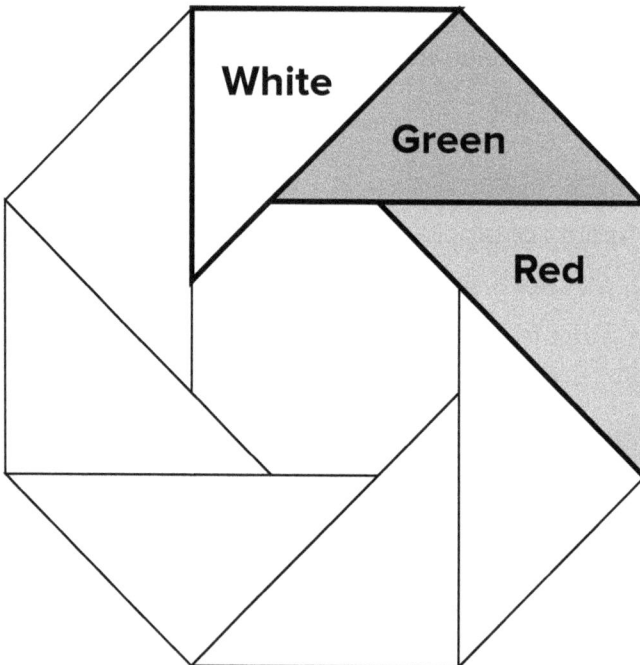

Color – Blue

(Calm, Order, Reliability, Harmony)

C H A P T E R 5

Patience, You're A Winner

When you're feeling downhearted, look up toward the heavens and see the marvelous hues of **blue** majesty in the skies.

....

You are a winner! Do not allow the stumbling blocks and obstacles to move you off the path you are heading on. But I cannot leave you with this statement because there are times when the obstacles are just what we need to move us in the right direction. What the enemy meant for evil, God meant for good.

PATIENCE, YOU'RE A WINNER

You can never lose with following your heart as you tune into God for guidance. Patience doesn't come easy for anyone, but waiting for the green light of pursuit will move you toward the prize. And as you are pursuing and pressing on with complete harmony, you will reach the goal.

Wherever you find yourself in life, on the job, or volunteering at a church or charitable organization, there will always be someone who challenges your style or becomes envious of you, and most of the time, their envy has no solid justification. Honestly, it could be about the way you look, talk, or handle situations and life. I have found that most green-eyed monsters are just unhappy with themselves, and if they can bring unhappiness into your world, they will do just that. It's as if they are looking for the weakest link in your chain of life to attempt a coup and seize control of your assets.

But you have a mission in which you must be able to recognize the offenders and intentionally put a plan in place to combat them. However, don't fall off the wagon that is taking you to your destination, believing everyone has a chip on their shoulder because of you. This is simply not true. There are good people and managers who turn into mentors and are genuinely looking out for you and your future. These managers or mentors have been where you are and understand what it will take to get you to your next level. When you find that great manager or mentor, cherish and thank them.

Little patience can be compared to a thief in the night who comes to take when everyone is sleeping and at their most vulnerable. Don't allow the thief to steal your joy, goals, ambitions, creativity, and other healthy qualities. Guard your heart and thoughts. Everyone is not aware of your backstory, and they have no clue as to how you got to where you are.

They do not know the tears and sacrifices that you poured out to water and the cultivation you've done to create the beautiful garden they see today. A garden takes time, and the vibrant colors that come with the small seed that was planted are awe-inspiring. There are the initial preparation and the tilling of the soil, additives to enrich the soil, seeds of sacrifice, watering, and daily tending to remove weeds that try to choke out the beauty that emerges from hard work and dedicated attention to detail. So, you find yourself relentlessly and persistently focused on what the future will look like once this garden has come to full fruition. And when harvest time comes, you will pick from the best of your garden, display the work of your hands, and enjoy the fruit of your labor, at times sharing and blessing someone else from the garden.

Remember, you didn't come to the garden alone. There's a wonderful hymn:

And He walks with me

And He talks with me

And He tells me I am His own

And the joy we share as we tarry there

None other has ever known.

In all your times of trouble and times when you're putting in the work, He is with you. Sometimes, recognizing this truth means putting your best effort in and then waiting for Him to bring results. We reap what we sow and those results will be a favorable harvest.

"Give, and it shall be given unto you; good measure, pressed down, and shaken together and running over, shall men give into your bosom. For with the same measure that ye mete withal it shall be measured to you again" (Luke 6:38, KJV).

Imagine this narrative: Your manager asks where you see yourself moving next within the company. You think about it and comment that you enjoy your present position, which you pretty much created. It has opened doors and allowed you to be exposed to a diverse customer base internally and externally. However, there is a shortfall in your department. You suggest a solution and continue to explain that if your idea were implemented, it would expand your current responsibilities and add increased value to the organization.

So innocent and trusting with the creative gifts that have been bestowed in your life, you reveal a new potential layer to your current position. Now the caveat to this new role is that you have literally been performing it all along. But you didn't possess the title to support your ongoing efforts.

Now, believing that sharing your vision will work in your behalf, you submit the documentation as requested to support the new change. Interestingly, after submission, you are advised that this type of position or new layer won't be possible within the company. The company is not interested in moving toward this type of organizational structure. A position like this would be best obtained outside the company, and you are encouraged to pursue it. You respond with a thank you and continue performing your job.

Then a curveball is thrown: they suggest you consider taking some classes, and if this type of role becomes available at the company, you'll be able to apply. Wait a minute. Back up. Earlier you were told the company was not interested and would not move in that direction. But now you're being told it could be to your advantage if you decide to pursue this role outside the company. This additional layer of education could be helpful on your resume. Hmm . . . is something going on here?

Our narrative gets better. This is not the first time you've faced a comment like this, a manager suggesting you look outside the company for your creative new position.

I can attest that early in my tenure, a manager warned me that he thought it would be best for me to begin searching for employment at another company. Why, you ask? Because I refused to go along with wrongful and continuously demeaning treatment of other employees. But I tend to digress because I have many life experiences and stories that I could share with you.

Back to the narrative.

You were asked for your thoughts about moving up the ladder, and now here comes a thief in the night. What thief, you say? The thief who takes your suggested new role and documentation, makes minor changes, and implements them within the organization. What do you do? Who do you turn to? Can anyone help you?

I hear you saying, "I'm going to fight back and confront that thief." Believe me, that's exactly what some people would do, and I totally get it. Your next reaction is anger, frustration, and a feeling of total betrayal.

Can I be open with you? I can relate to this narrative because I experienced it.

As I was pouring out my heart to the Lord and tears were streaming down my face in prayer, a girlfriend who was not aware of the situation sent me a text message. It said "Trust God" with an image of Jesus holding a large teddy bear behind His back. A little girl stood across from Him with a small teddy bear behind her back. With His hand extended, He was saying to her, "Trust me." At that moment I found true peace and willingly gave this situation to my Heavenly Father. During the time of prayer, an answer was already provided to me.

You see, I had to believe this was a small-teddy-bear experience compared to what God has in store for me. This was not an easy transition because in the next few days, this bad experience reared its ugly head, reminding me of what had just occurred. But the word of God ignited within me, strengthening me and giving me confidence. We know that God has a plan for our lives according to Jeremiah 29:11 (NIV): *"For I know the plans I have for you,' declares the Lord, plans to prosper you and not to harm you, plans to give you hope and a future.'"*

So, what comes next in this story—forgiveness? Oh, it takes time to work through this process. But it is so worth it in the end. Don't retaliate, don't stop being kind, and don't stop being you. Let it go because if it was a part of your future, it would be yours. Trust me, no one can take God's promises that are stockpiled for you, stored in the warehouse of heaven, waiting to be distributed.

Friends, sometimes we must forgo the small teddy bears of life and trust God has a bigger, better, brighter plan, an enormous teddy bear for us. It's not easy to accept and it may take time to believe things will be better on the other side of the situation. Oh, but when your faith is awakened as a new day arises and brand-new mercy is given, it doesn't take a lot to believe—just mustard-seed-sized faith is all you need. God will make it up to you no matter how treacherous the storm or battle. It will pass, and victory will be yours. Don't give up on your dreams, stay encouraged, and walk by faith and not by sight.

Journey Pause:

Life is good despite its high and low times. As you progress through those moments, allow the color blue into your space. I understand at times it can be quite difficult, but think on the good things that life has given. Focus on them even when bad seems to take a demanding stance, swallowing and stealing the harmony and order that blue brings.

Blue is the color of calm, order, reliability, and harmony. There will be times when you just need to draw from the sensation of the color palette of blue.

Patience is a virtue and can be advantageous as you journey through this sometimes-unpredictable world. No one likes to wait because we live in a world where everything is instant, fast, quick, and to-go. But sometimes we need to allow things to marinate and slow cook to allow the flavors to come together. You will learn that order is a welcome atmosphere as you wait patiently for the next move in your life. Stay in a calm place even when chaos is all around.

Crossroad Enlightenment: Calm (Patience)

"Love is patient, love is kind. It does not envy, it does not boast, it is not proud. It does not dishonor others, it is not self-seeking, it is not easily angered, it keeps no record of wrongs" (1 Corinthians 13:4–5, NIV).

Note: It's the end of the chapter, and we are adding blue to the design. We now have white, green, red, and blue octagon symbols. Let's keep building.

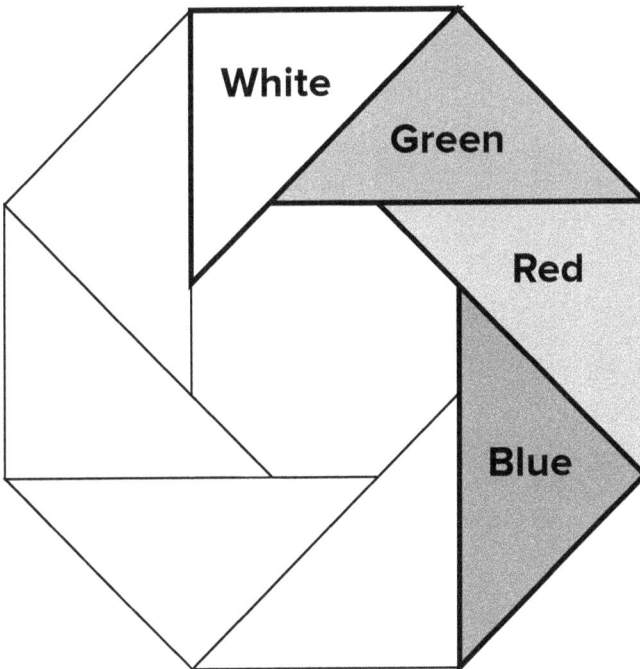

Color – Orange

(Cheerful, Warm, Social, Playful, Exotic, Spicy)

C H A P T E R   6

You Are Unique

With the end of the day a sunset arrayed in **orange** gradually interchanges with blue to take control of the skies.

....

You may say, "I don't consider myself unique. My style, talents, and gifts are no different from anyone else's." This response is not strange because most people don't see themselves as different, except for their obvious exterior appearance. However, in addition to the exterior, the interior is also different. You see, you really are special, and it is an honor to be peculiar and set apart.

Everyone who has been given the breath of life is uniquely created by God. The Bible states in 1 Peter 2:9 (KJV), *"But ye are a chosen generation, a royal priesthood, an holy nation, a peculiar people; that ye should show forth the praises of him who hath called you out of darkness into his marvellous light."* You are part of a chosen generation. Merriam-Webster. com Dictionary describes the word *unique* as meaning the only one of its kind, unlike anything else, or particularly remarkable, special or unusual.

If we look back in the Bible, there is a story about a young man who had dreams. His father, who loved him, gave him a coat of many colors. What made this coat special was that it was uniquely fashioned just for him. He had other siblings, but none of them were blessed by the father with a stunning colorful coat. This gift, as prominent as it was, belonged to Joseph and to him alone. I believe if one of the other siblings had attempted to steal or try on the coat, they would have found out it didn't fit. The coat was crafted with love for one person only, and that person was Joseph.

You and I have also been given a coat of many colors. That coat could represent your organizational skills, your creative thoughts, your business savvy, your ability to work with people, your style of dress, your vision and how it is executed, and the list goes on. Your coat sets you apart from the crowd and intimidates those around you, like Joseph's brothers. Instead of moving closer to you to gain insight, they at times hate, envy, talk about, and even persecute you for the beautiful coat you wear. A coat, may I say, that was made exclusively for you and belongs to you. A coat that didn't require any assistance from you.

I have had occasions to be extremely specific about this unique gifting that we each hold. For example, I am not a very patient person when it comes to assembling anything. First, I do not like it. I find it challenging and honestly a waste of time. The idea of following this piece of paper with specific directions is almost mind-blowing and so arduous. However, my sister and some friends can open the box of loose parts and get excited about the challenge that is ahead. I have watched them strategically place the pieces in some strange type of order, and the killer part is they do not look at the directions. If they do, it's a quick overview to ensure a part is not missing.

Who are these people, and where did they get this patience and talent from? They are the Josephs of the world with a unique quality that sets them apart. Should you be jealous of their gifts? Absolutely not. However, you should honor their giftings and home in on their skill sets. This is an area in which you build great businesses and corporations based on individual skills and talents. Bring those skills and talents together, and what a powerful organization you can build.

Honestly, my feeling is that things should be pre-assembled when they reach my home, ready for immediate use, but that's not always realistic.

During the pandemic of 2020, everyone was literally sheltering in place, and during that time I was working remotely. Life as we once knew it changed right before our eyes and we were forced to perform life differently. For me that meant working from home as a remote employee. I lived in a split-level home with stairs, but that did not satisfy the yearning to keep moving and be active. So, I purchased an exercise bike via the TV. The host of the program where I saw the bike explained that assembling it would take no more than twenty minutes. He dismantled it several times, showing how easy assembly would be once it reached your home. I thought, okay, I can do this, and ordered the bike. Well, remember, I am not keen on reading the white paper filled with step-by-step directions. But I had to change my thinking and take on a new Goliath.

Sometimes life and circumstances will cause you to take a closer look at yourself and make critical changes in order to get what you want and need. And of course, what I wanted was another resource to get some much-needed exercise. Within seven business days, the long, brown thirty-pound box was delivered to my front door, and I could almost feel the anxiety. Why did I purchase this? I thought about a friend who could have this bike assembled in the allotted time of twenty minutes. I called my sister, who is the queen of assembly, and she gave me a pep talk of encouragement and advised me to take my time and read those dreaded directions.

So, I rolled up my sleeves and said, "Kitty, you can do this." I sat on the chair with my reading glasses and focused on the step-by-step directions. I even had to read some areas more than once—honestly, I read some parts three or four times and out loud. I used tools I have never used before and seemed to draw skills and insight from some unknown storehouse with new skills on a shelf, waiting for me to pull from the inventory.

You see, there are times when we think we cannot accomplish the task presented to us due to insufficient experience, skills, or talents. But that day I was led to a take the shovel of courage, dig deep within myself, and uncover the hidden treasures that I had no idea I possessed. Treasures of patience, commitment, building skills, and more.

So many times, we miss opportunities, promotions, new experiences, and other benefits because we have told ourselves, "I cannot do this; I do not have the abilities to perform this task; I am not talented enough, pretty enough, good enough, strong enough, wise enough to take on this new adventure that may change my entire life." We allow fear to take over and grip us, stopping us from moving forward.

Have you ever heard someone say, "I can't wear that color. It's so wrong for me"? Well, the question to ask yourself is, have you tried it, or are you assuming it won't work? Or did you allow someone to put that concept in your psyche?

People love to tell us what we should and should not do based on their own experiences or, in most cases, just to stop us from moving past them. In other words, they attempt to hold you back. But we do not have to experience everything in 100-percent doses. If we take on the full dose, it could possibly ruin us for life. So, sometimes the prescription calls for a lesser dose that will still get the job done slowly and steadily, taking a step at a time as you move along this journey.

I am sure you have met people who are talented in areas that are challenging to you and vice versa. I am sure your areas of strength are seen by others as daunting. You see, this is what makes us so unique and yet peculiar in our own special way. These talents and skills can lead to invisible intimidation, which can rear its ugly head, and we can find ourselves being overlooked or looked at with envy by those who feel inadequate after comparing themselves to us. Why do we compare ourselves to others?

I have several stories that I could share regarding invisible intimidation. You really do not see it initially; however, as you pursue your goals through life, it will exhibit itself with a testimony attached.

For example, I remember being told by my immediate manager that I sometimes came across as a know-it-all. I stated, "I don't know everything, but what I do know, I know." He wanted me to back down from the confidence I had in doing my job to my best ability in pursuit of excellence. Invisible intimidation lifted its ugly head that day.

Now, allow me to give you a little background on a particular senior manager. He was, without a doubt, an individual who could intimidate people just with his presence. When he visited an office, the ambience changed like a roaring lion had come in, seeking whom he may devour. Those with good eyesight and any sense of feeling felt the shift in the atmosphere. People almost looked as if they were tiptoeing so the lion wouldn't know of their presence.

However, I was not moved by this individual and the bullying spirit he possessed. It all came to a screeching halt one day when he challenged my way of handling a project. Please understand the demand in question from him to me was that an amenity was not needed. However, I explained that the amenity was a part of a standard package deal. Even if it were removed, the cost would remain the same because it was included in the package. Well, he did not appreciate my response. Now understand, I was not disrespectful in my email responses, only honestly trying to explain the process and final decision to him. But when you're dealing with someone who feels they know it all and their title brings entitlement, nothing you say or do will change their mind. It becomes a losing battle, a battle you did not initiate and one you probably won't win.

My immediate manager who also feared this senior manager, pushed back and placed the blame on me, stating I should have picked up the phone and called the senior manager versus using email. I replied that I had responded according to the senior manager's means of communication. If he had wanted to talk, he could have picked up the phone and spoken to me. But because others bowed to his folly of control and I did not, it took this senior manager to another level. From that day forward, I felt as if I had been placed on a hit list—the list that we all know exists but at times wish to ignore. It was all due to the confidence I exhibited, not fearing him or disrespecting him but standing my ground on what was factual and my values. So, this incident placed me in a category of arrogance in their eyes because I remained steadfast about the actualities. How do you change what cannot be changed?

Be ready for those office or school bullies who attempt to steal your joy and peace. Refuse to accept their sometimes-subtle attempts to discredit you or make you think twice about what you know to be true. And don't be alarmed or surprised if others don't come to your defense. It's hard to have allies when fear is in the room, and it will seem as if you are standing alone in the middle of the circle, surrounded by a bully and those who fear him. But remember, there is a God who sits high and looks low. He is the only ally you will ever need. He will go before you and fight your battles because those battles belong to Him.

After our conversation, my immediate manager said, "I'm not asking you to change."

I told him, "You don't have to worry about that. I will not." I continued with what I said at the beginning of this conversation: "I don't know everything, but what I know, I know, and I'm good at it."

In the end, walk in your uniqueness, but remember that you must be able to dwell and live with the uniqueness in others as well. This is not a one-man show and you are not the only one who is unique. Whether we perceive someone as good or bad, they are still unique. So, stop trying to fit in and be someone you are not. Stop the molding process that attempts to bring you under their subjection. Don't vacate the calling on your life and abandon the post assigned to you, thinking if you can just look or act like someone else, all will be good or if you side with a bully or naysayer, your life will be better. Believe me, it's a trick, and it won't work for your good.

No matter your color style, we must respect those we walk, work, and live with daily. Put jealousy aside, appreciate the uniqueness that has been bestowed on others, and try to figure out how your uniqueness can contribute to the success of the company and the world. Figure out how your uniqueness can mesh with someone else's to create something beautiful. Do your best to live peaceably with all men, understanding that it may be a challenge, but you can lean in and press toward it.

Step up with your color style, stand tall with confidence, and treat your neighbor with respect, providing a smile because we are all equal with our style.

So just Color Your Style and be proud of who God made you to be. Hold your head up with your unique self. Go for it—there will never be another person like you!

Journey Pause:

Do you like spicy foods such as habanero peppers and buffalo wings, or do you slather your food with hot sauce? As you know, there is an instant reaction when the spices meet the tongue, then the body reacts with tiny water beading on the brow called sweat, and now the hand begins to wave back and forth, trying to bring some relief with a wind of coolness.

Orange is **cheerful**, yet **warm**, **social**, oh so playful, magically **exotic**, hot, and **spicy**. It is a powerful color that is not normally worn or used by many people. My mother loved orange so much that our sectional sofa in our home was orange. What a powerful statement it made when anyone entered our living room. It showed that here was a woman who was confident in who she was and how she wanted her home represented.

There will be times when orange is needed to usher in happiness, add spiciness to a dull atmosphere or situation, or be a healer. Did you know we envision vitamin C in the color orange? Wow, how healthy is that? It's the color of transition, moving you from sickness to wholeness. Allow it to be a partner in your life as the heat from habaneros and feel free to extinguish it with the hues of blue or green if it becomes overpowering.

So, get ready to shift to the next move in your life. By now you understand that you are unique— there is not another person like you. You are so special that you cannot be duplicated. But trust me, there will be people who will try to discourage you and some who will just dislike you because of your social, cheery, spicy, determined uniqueness. Oh, but you keep being who you were created to be.

Crossroad Enlightenment: Cheerful

"A cheerful disposition is good for your health; gloom and doom leave you done-tired" (Proverbs 17:22, MSG).

Note: It's the end of the chapter, and we are adding orange to the design. We now have white, green, red, blue, and orange octagon symbols. Let's keep building.

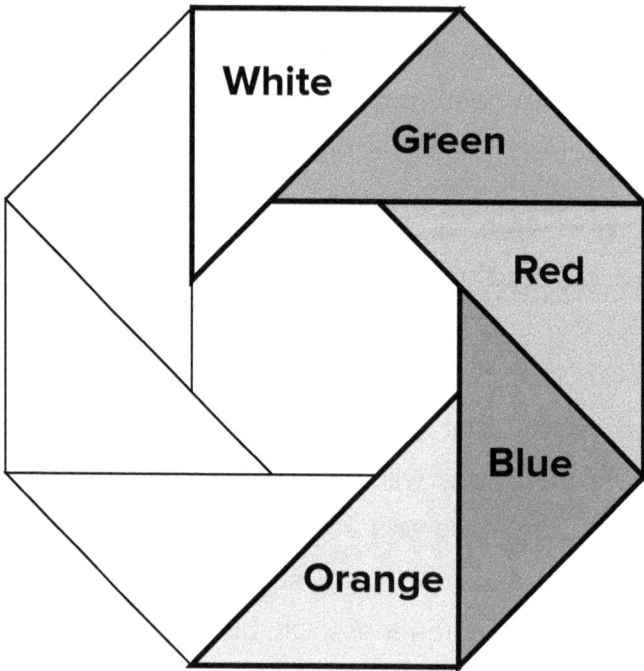

Color – Black

(Sophisticated, Artistic, Powerful, Sensitive,
Meticulous, Mysterious)

CHAPTER 7

Define Your World

Morning, noon, and then night—**black** dictates the night
skies, allowing the twinkling of the suspended stars and
moon to perform against its backdrop.

....

You play an important part in defining your future in the
world we live in. It is noted that our future has already
been defined and we are literally walking toward it day by day.
"For we walk by faith, not by sight" (2 Corinthians 5:7, KJV).

But we must do our part and be bold in how we shape, form and mold this piece of clay that is you. You can allow others to create your future, or you can roll up your sleeves, get your hands messy and take the lead.

Leaders do not always have to lead people, but they surrender to the Master Builder in creating their own destiny. So, in some sense we all have leadership traits; it just depends on who you are leading.

It takes patience to gain tenure in any job or life assignment. You must make up your mind to stay in it for the long haul. Decide that whatever it takes, you're all in. Roll up your sleeves, take a solid stance, stick your chest out like Superman, and move into what is coming next.

Whatever direction life leads you in, it will be worth it in the end. You see, all experiences, whether good or bad, help us as we move to the next level of our lives. I have learned that when things come easy, it is only because there are some past experiences and nuggets you draw from to make it through. We glean from the fragments of our past.

Yes, past experiences are steps on the road of life. It is like following the yellow brick road, only each stone on the road has a different outcome and effect on your journey. Some steps bring joy, yet others bring frustration, some bring exhaustion and a desire to quit, and then there are the smooth, easy ones that make you think, how did I ease on down the road so smoothly? Something must be wrong. So, you doubt your walk and begin to look back at the path you've traveled to see if a stone was missed along the way.

No stone was missed, but all stones do not have to bring challenges, tears, or defeat. That's because life is not always going to be difficult. So, when we rest and step on the easy stones, we can thank God for the stones of victory that lead to the next big rock or mountain we will face.

But remember, we can look at the mountains in our life, look at them squarely, boldly, and say, "Move out of my way." We speak to them by faith, not doubting in our hearts, but believing what we say will come true and we will have it. You have this promise—just open your mouth and believe in your heart.

There is a residual effect of God's blessings, not only on you but on others whom you encounter. Your lifestyle and the way you conduct yourself, your handling of positive and negative situations, pour into those secret, invisible folks whom you are mentoring, and you do not even realize the impact you have on their lives. You may never speak to them personally or have a relationship, but they see you. They see the way you handle the obstacles, and often the way you are treated is in plain view.

But I am reminded of two individuals who were beaten and thrown into prison before an angry mob because they chose to conduct themselves in a godly manner. Oh, but at midnight, Paul and Silas encouraged themselves while in chains, bruised, and bloody, and while being watched by a host of guards. They sang praises and worshipped the God of their salvation. The earth began to shake, the prison doors swung open, and the chains were broken. Freedom was theirs to take, and it was there for the other prisoners who were experiencing this awesome miracle. But Paul and Silas chose to stand still and be examples to the other prisoners. These two mentors left some residual effects of God's blessings. When the guard knew for sure every prisoner had fled, Paul spoke up and said, "We are all here."

I'm sure that as the days went on, the prisoners who'd had an opportunity to experience that spectacular day were changed forever. They were changed not only by what they saw but by the God to whom Paul and Silas sang praises and prayed, the one who opened the prison doors.

You and I can also leave residual effects of God's blessing on those we encounter or those who observe us as secret spies from afar. Do you not know our lives are being judged daily by peers, coworkers, our children, and others? Our responsibility is not to please the onlookers but to be an example or template so they can begin to mold their lives in a positive fashion. There seems to be a tendency to emulate good, positive behavior. However, infrequent bad behavior isn't the top choice for most to exhibit.

We are the light of the world, a city that sits on a hill and cannot be hidden. When we act out in a way that is contrary to the Word, it can leave a lingering effect, but not the kind we want to leave that represents the God we serve.

The path is open to all who are willing to get on it and take the first steps toward success and freedom. Come and experience a world that is waiting for all the beautiful gifts, talents, creativity, and innovative ideas you will bring to the table of life. Someone needs a mentor, and you just might be the one who can help propel them to new heights and deeper depths.

Your style— "Color My Style" is waiting to be revealed!

Journey Pause:

The color black is **sophisticated** (classy, cultured, refined), **artistic** (creative, inventive, imaginative), **powerful** (influential, dominant, strong), **sensitive** (thoughtful, sympathetic, caring), **meticulous** (accurate, discerning, detailed), **mysterious** (secretive, strange, peculiar).

We have all experienced the characteristics of black in our lifestyle. I would like to urge you to utilize the color black on your personal journey. Immerse yourself in it during certain life stages to be fearless, powerful, and strong, and then in other times to be sensitive, caring, discerning, a little secretive, and strange to those around you.

You can't disclose your journey of life to everyone; there must be some areas that are sacred to you and your Creator. Some things are not to be revealed until their time. Can you imagine exposing a dream, before you have prayed and strategically planned, to someone who just might steal your idea? However, there are times of being sensitive and caring toward others who are in need, which is so important. For example, being accurate and detail-oriented can avert a financial disaster. How about being discerning, which could drive a business into immediate success with its clientele? A happy client is a returning client who also tells others.

Crossroad Enlightenment: Powerful

"For the Spirit God gave us does not make us timid, but gives us power, love and self-discipline" (2 Timothy 1:7, NIV).

Note: It's the end of the chapter, and we are adding black to the design. We now have white, green, red, blue, orange, and black octagon symbols. Let's keep building.

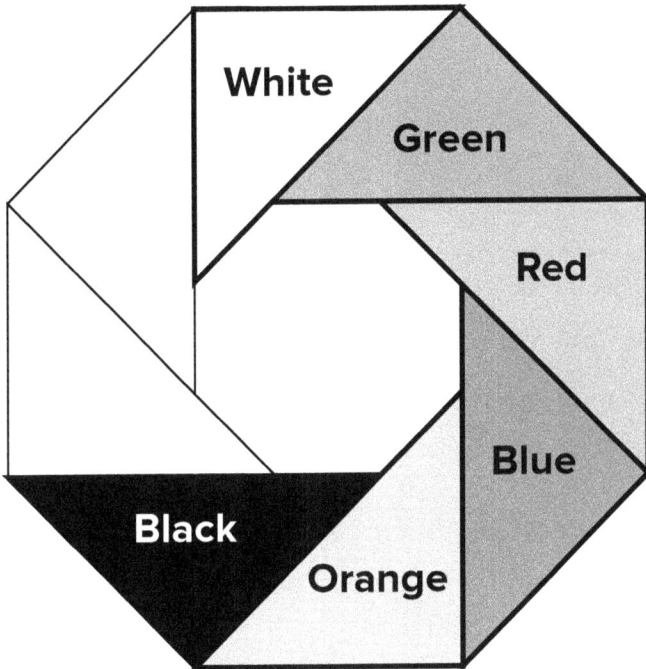

Color – Purple

(Vibrant, royal, eccentric, rich, unique, artistic)

C H A P T E R   8

Empowered To Attain

And His train fills the temple as the King of Kings moves into the room with His royal robe of bright, brilliant **purple** adorned with a crown of jewels sparkling upon His head. Give Him glory!

....

You have conquered and overcome the obstacles, naysayers, haters, backbiters, and others who stood in your path. Now it is time to define your world in a whole new way.

I now empower you to bring life to your current mindset and unique style. It is time to believe in yourself and move toward that deep gut feeling of where your next move will be. It is like a heavy burden, and you cannot get this thought out of your mind that there is more to life than what you are living right now. You feel a slight push to press forward, step out of your comfort zone, and spring forth.

It is the symphony of color that moves and encourages. As musical notes are to a musician or to a symphony of instruments, each one brings forth a new sound, and combined they create something wonderful, soothing, calming, and even exciting. So is color to the soul of man, pushing us toward our goals and purpose. Vibrantly, it seeks opportunities and opens doors for us to walk through.

Remember, no two people are alike. Your style is uniquely yours.

You are what you think, do, say, and achieve.

Think

"Let this mind be in you, which was also in Christ Jesus" (Philippians 2:5, KJV). The way we think will motivate our next move, and the way we treat others will last a lifetime. The patience and willingness to wait and believe better days are on the way are priceless.

Stop thinking the thing you want is not for you, but only for others. Put aside negative thoughts like it is not for me, I cannot do this, I do not have what it takes, I am not talented enough, I do not have the financial wherewithal, I am too old, or nothing ever works out for me. The mind is a powerful weapon, and it can bring us to our purpose or leave us on the path alone, afraid, and lifeless to go forward. Stomp on fear. Speak to it, tell it to move out of your way, and unleash the boldness of confidence. Stop looking to people to validate you or your dreams.

As we maneuver along the paths of success, we can think on these things, as the Bible states.

"Think of yourselves the way Christ Jesus thought of himself. He had equal status with God but didn't think so much of himself that he had to cling to the advantages of that status no matter what. Not at all. When the time came, he set aside the privileges of deity and took on the status of a slave, became human! *Having become human, he stayed human. It was an incredibly humbling process. He didn't claim special privileges. Instead, he lived a selfless, obedient life and then died a selfless, obedient death—and the worst kind of death at that—a crucifixion"*(Philippians 2:5–8, MSG).

Do

It is time to move toward opportunities. As the old principle says, actions speak louder than words. Sometimes we need to just act and not speak so much. Speaking to the wrong people can deter us from where we are supposed to be focusing our time and attention. Believe me, you can't trust everyone with the promise God has shown you. Stop acting like it is for everyone but you. Opportunity belongs to all of us. There is enough in the world for all of us to grab our piece of the pie. Some of us must push a little harder to obtain it, but it is ours for the taking. Get moving and act on the promise that is yours and yours only.

I clearly remember when I was asked a simple but complex question about my next move in life. I had just completed a written exam that I did not pass, and I was feeling defeated and not too smart. As I walked out of the lonely, gray-walled testing room toward the test administrator's desk, she stopped what she was doing, looked at me, and said with sincerity, "Now when are you going to write that book? You have a story to tell?"

I looked around to see who she was talking to, but there was no one behind me. So I guessed she must be speaking to me, and I sheepishly laughed out loud. But, after I laughed, something hit me, something was resurrected inside of me, and I said to myself, this is the missing piece. You say, what missing piece? Well, I had attempted to start a small business five years prior, but I had felt there was something missing. A website and PowerPoint presentation were created, a wonderful banner was designed with my logo, and I had purchased tablecloths and created a bright, bold centerpiece for the registration table and flyers to promote my message.

But what I thought was a clear direction, a clear vision, was not. In other words, I didn't have the full scope of what God was preparing for me. So I ceased, took a step back, and placed the vision on hold!

I spoke at a women's conference, received good feedback, and even took on a client. But there was this empty, lingering feeling of nothingness. Something is missing, I thought. This is not it. So, I placed this dream on the altar for clarity. You know, I put the promise, the vision, the one that I knew God had given me, on a semi-shelf. But it was never far from me because I carried the fractional vision with me. As a matter of fact, I carried it in a bright yellow folder with a smiley face on the cover that said, "Smile, God loves you." And in my heart, I believed a revelation would soon be granted to me. But the revelation didn't come in the next year, or the second or third. It took approximately five years, during a pandemic, to hear the next step from the mouth of a stranger.

Sarah and Abraham were informed by the angel advising them that this time next year they would have a son, which was God's promise being fulfilled. I, like Sarah, laughed when I was asked, "When are you going to write that book?"

But when the time of revelation arrived, the joke was on me. Now who had the last laugh? God keeps his promises and in time, His time, they come to pass. Don't be surprised at how they are packaged. Just receive the gift and accelerate your progress toward excellence.

The Bible states, *"Dear children, let us not love with words or speech but with actions and in truth"* (1 John 3:18, NIV).

It may not initially look pleasing to the naked eye or the empty pockets you are trying to fill, but some things come by faith, prayer, and action (works). We look through a glass darkly, and until the light shines into the dark place, we cannot see what lies ahead. I have faced some dark areas in my life and thought many times about giving up, thinking the goal was not worth my time or energy. But there is always a still small voice that tells us to keep pressing toward the mark, holding onto the promises—this too shall pass, and it will get better. You are not in this alone.

Believe me, that annoying negative voice will pass, and one day, maybe out of nowhere, you will look up and see you have conquered and seized that mountain of negativity. Now you are standing flat-footed at the top of it. The warrior has won the battle.

Say

Speak and live truth in everything you do. It is not always easy along the path to success, but an honest individual will always come out on top of every situation. One lie will lead to another, and dishonesty will haunt you throughout your career and life. Speak truth, be about the right thing, and do not allow the pressure of peers or dollar signs to lead you away from what you know is right. Respect those you encounter along the way, even those who don't do the right thing and climb over the backs of others to reach their goals. All climbing does not lead to a good spot at the top, especially if the desired position is obtained by deceiving others, pilfering what clearly isn't yours, or mishandling people. These all lead to a lonely place at the top. We need each other to survive. No man is an island. Two minds are better than one.

I have had ideas robbed from me, but one thing is for sure: it did not work out for the thief because they did not have the passion for the idea or any insight into how it was inspired to carry it to fruition. Those who steal never come out on top. It may seem that they are winning, but believe me, there are no winners when someone takes something that was not conceived by them. You cannot birth something that was not embedded deep inside of you. What comes forth is defective, deficient, and malnourished.

Being steadfast and unmovable is a gift that empowers you to stay in place and win the top prize: the crown.

Achieve

Seniority is a blessing, and with the years under your belt, you are often looked upon as the expert in your field. You become the go-to person because of your knowledge and experience. The positions I've held with tenure on the job allowed me to become the go-to person not just for the assigned area I worked in but for other areas as well. When I entered the workforce, I was hired to perform a specific job.

However, as time passed and a level of comfort came, I began to expand my knowledge to other areas of the company. By the time I reached my twenty-fifth year of employment, I called myself the Google for the company because one thing was sure: if I didn't know the answer, I knew where to begin to find the answer. I was often contacted and told that someone had said, "If you don't know the answer, start with Kitty. She will know or tell you where to start." I am a retainer of notes as well as a human computer with downloaded information in my mind to help sort through queries and inquiries from my peers.

Ask yourself: Am I willing to explore and be open to learning new areas? Am I ready to move to uncharted territory? Can I work with other departments and managers, or am I stuck trying to be elevated in one area? We can become our own worst enemy and nightmare. Reaching toward something that will take a lifetime will slow your exposure to a variety of areas. Now, if you are not willing to be a steady, stable worker, this concept will not work for you. You see, being impatient can lead to destruction, and most of the time, hasty decisions don't work out for your good. Don't compromise—stand on what you believe and be committed.

For example, most likely you will not be hired as the CEO, and that is okay. However, if that is your long-term goal, go for it. But first get in the door, research opportunities, get to know your peers, and find out who holds certain positions. You may not know what you would like to initially work toward but begin somewhere. Navigate through the maze until you find the area that works for you. Tenure will lead you down the paths of opportunities and open your mind.

Exposure is your friend and can introduce you to new and exciting areas. Dabble in new interests, volunteer for assignments, be inquisitive, and store what you learn. It will come in handy one day when you reach back for those stored experiences.

Recognize that the Lord brings out the best in you! Be authentic to what you are called to do—Color Your Style! It does not have to look like anyone else's; it is uniquely yours and it belongs exclusively to you.

As you move down your path, you will be exposed to all colors. Your next move will depend heavily on how you choose to exhibit and color your style. There is no getting around being exposed to all colors. Remember, the world was created in colors. But it takes a mature attitude to step out of your comfort zone and deal with all colors and styles. Some colors clash and do not mix well. No problem—you just need to be confident in your color and style. Work with the colors that want to work with you. Don't get hung up on what matches and what doesn't. It's all about attitude, so make it happen. There's more than one way to do anything and always room to put a new spin on an old way.

Do we ever stop working toward a goal? I'm here to say no—never. Whether we are working full time, working part time, or retired, there will always be a mountain or path to conquer. Stay on the path, and by the time you reach the stage of retirement, you will have evolved into a supercharged conqueror with many medals and trophies on your shelf of accomplishments and will have been exposed to all types of colors. But don't get it twisted—retiring doesn't mean you stop pursuing goals. What it means is that you now have control of your time to spend it on what you deem important. Your knowledge is gold, and it can help guide the next generation. Don't keep that knowledge to yourself.

And remember how we talked about the stories and world experiences we gain from our parents, grandparents, teachers, and mentors? You now have your own stories to tell the next generation. That's what I'm doing right now: telling my stories and sharing my colorful life's journey to ensure someone else will not make the same mistakes. The stones of life, as you step on them, can be made not challenging but easy because you heard from someone who told their story. Let us pass on our stories and the colors we have encountered or adapted to our lives to help to make this world a better place, even if it is just by one person at a time.

Look at sharing your story as similar to how the Good Samaritan, who was walking toward his destination, took the time to stop and help someone in need. He had the ability to reach out to someone in distress and in trouble while others walked by. He used what he had to extend kindness to a stranger. He allowed his style to stretch out to someone else, touching this man in a way that he would never forget.

At times we may face a stranger as we walk along the path of life. How will you react to their situation or pain? That pain could inspire you to train or mentor a coworker whom others refuse to assist. Can you be the sponsor to someone who doesn't look like you but clearly has the skills to perform the task? Or to a mother in the grocery store who is struggling to find additional cash to pay for much-needed food for her family? Or to someone being abused who has scars as proof, or on whom you see the abusive acts being performed? And the list could go on. But the question to you is, will you be able to give and look past what others walk past? It's like saying, "I see you—do you see me?"

Your style will be challenged, but you must stand your ground and choose to be you with dignity, courage, faith, and color! Don't run from the challenges, but stand flat-footed look life in the eyes, and fight on. Believe me, you will be the topic of many conversations. But try to see it as good because you have blocked them from criticizing someone else.

This fight may bring you to a place in which you have to pause. Life circumstances, such as a divorce from the love of your life, the death of a precious family member, the loss of a job or income you thought was secure, a sibling rivalry, children's issues, personal illness, can bring you to a temporary stop. These things can lead you to a place of emptiness and uncertainty where you wonder which direction to take down this highway of life. This is the time to take the next exit, step back, reassess, take it to the Lord in prayer, and decide which path you will take to Color Your Style.

Journey Pause:

Do you ever feel like royalty? Do you understand just how special and loved you are?

Let's look at the liberating color **purple**. It represents being **vibrant** (alive), **royal** (majestic), **eccentric** (peculiar), **rich** (valuable), **unique** (irreplaceable), and **artistic** (creative).

Please allow me to give you a little something to smile about: you and I are part of a chosen generation, a royal priesthood. We are alive, peculiar, oh so valuable, irreplaceable, and yet creative in our own right. So, on those days when you are feeling inadequate and defeated, thinking you're all alone, draw from the color purple. Remember who you are and the promises prearranged for you. Whatever God has promised, it will come to pass!

Crossroad Enlightenment: Unique

"With your very own hands you formed me; now breathe your wisdom over me so I can understand you. When they see me waiting, expecting your Word, those who fear you will take heart and be glad" (Psalm 119:73–74, MSG).

It's the end of the chapter, and we are adding purple to the design. We now have white, green, red, blue, orange, black, and purple octagon symbols. Let's keep building.

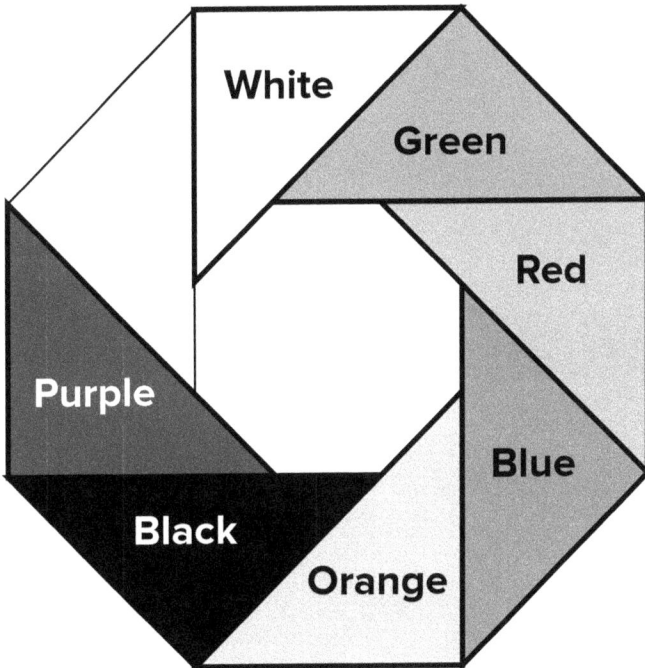

It Resides within You

(All Colors)

C H A P T E R   9

Color My Style

When the rainstorm ceases, a beautiful reminder of God's awesomeness appears in a rainbow. All colors unite in agreement, extending toward the heavens.

....

As we end this journey, I hope it is clear to you that Color My Style begins internally and will project externally. What's inside of you, what resides within you, and what you hold dear—your self-awareness, strength, determination, compassion, creativity, and even courage—establish your unique style.

At times, the internal activity stored up comes alive externally and a real outpouring of who you are, deeply rooted in faith, grace, and peace, springs forth in color. Whatever is placed in your path of life and the way you see yourself will determine how you see your future. We have been given a promise in Jeremiah 29:11 (NIV): *"'For I know the plans I have for you,' declares the Lord, 'plans to prosper you and not to harm you, plans to give you hope and a future.'"*

A plan that will not harm you but give you hope and a future should make you put on your running shoes and take off toward your purpose and destiny. There will never be another one like you.

Isaiah 40:29–31 (NIV) states, *"He gives strength to the weary and increases the power of the weak. Even youths grow tired and weary, and young men stumble and fall; but those who hope in the Lord will renew their strength. They will soar on wings like eagles; they will run and not grow weary, they will walk and not be faint."*

Do you realize that our God was the first in uniqueness? He's the Alpha and Omega, the beginning and the end. There's no one like Him, no one compares to Him, no one can replace Him, and there's no point in trying to compete against Him. He is the ultimate unique, one, and only Savior, the ruler and creator of this world. Glory to God!

So, if our God is unique, what makes you think he did not make you unique, exceptional, rare, irreplaceable, or even peculiar?

Be proud of who you are no matter your ethnicity, which is filled with beauty, your upbringing filled with love, or your present state in this life filled with promises. It is time to rise up, take your rightful place, transform your thinking, and be renewed. Be renewed with a deeper determination not to allow anything or anyone to impact or stop where God is leading you. Only you can allow the obstacles or challenges of life to deter you from your destiny and dreams. Dream big and dream large. It is up to you to Color Your Style.

"In all your ways acknowledge Him, and He shall direct your paths" (Proverbs 3:6, NKJV).

It's the end of the chapter, and look what we have built. All the colors unify to create this design. We have white, green, red, blue, orange, black, and purple octagon symbols. Could we add more? Absolutely. All it takes is to keep building. Knock down the walls that try to divide us and construct new ways of cohesion.

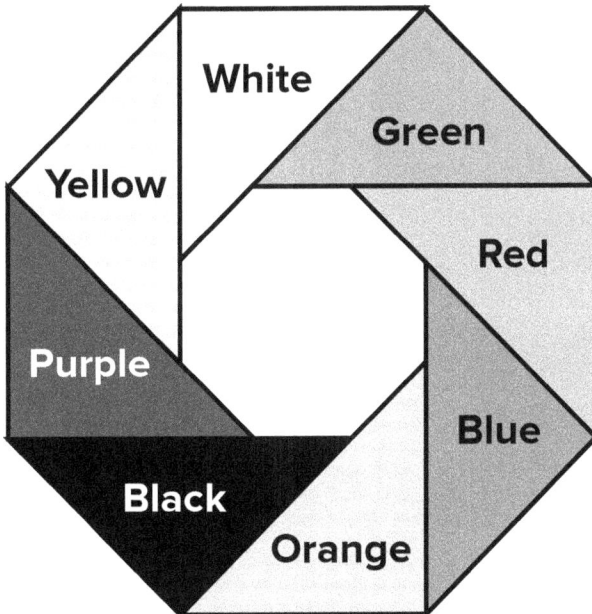

CHAPTER 10

We All Win - Let's Stand Together

We all win!

Every color is equal. Every color brings forth value that is precious. Every color completes the canvas of life. Every color reigns supreme in its own unique way. When you mixed the hues, a new creation begins. A new gift of color is created. Every color comes from God, who is no respecter of person. He is the creator; He is the ultimate artist, and we are seeing through His vision in color.

How can you live in this world and not see color? You cannot run from it, nor can you hide from it or destroy it. When you close your eyes, you see color. When you open your eyes, it appears again. It is everywhere, ever present and never fading into the sunset. Ah, the sunset . . . how beautifully the colors seem to dance and tangle together as the sun comes to rest for the day. The glory of the moon and stars that light the darkness in an intimate love story end the day. A new day appears with the morning, and the bright sun now takes full authority and commands the day.

Oh, my friends, can you understand the wondrous works of our Lord and how He allow color to bring beauty to this world? Beauty that you proudly display, living and walking confidently in your uniqueness. There will never be another one like you. You are special! I will keep saying it until you get it. You are special!

No one can kill, steal, or destroy the unique color that belongs to you, and you only. Stand proud, stand tall, in who you are designed to be. You add color to the backdrop of life. You bring in a perspective that no one else can contribute. You shine in your own special, matchless way. You help to complete the rainbow that adorns this canvas of life. You must stop thinking less of yourself and believe God makes no mistakes. The only mistake is not appreciating who you were created to be.

You never walk alone. Bring your best self, your color, to the table that is spread before you. Take your assigned seat, give thanks, and take your rightful place in this world of great opportunities. It is yours for the taking as you show respect for the vast array of colors waiting for their turn to shine and be revealed. What God has for you—it is for you. And what he has for others belongs to them. So, you don't have to covet, steal, or overshadow others to illuminate your color style. Be proud of what has been given to you and hold it close and dear to your heart.

Uniqueness belongs to everyone. God created us with our own special uniqueness. It's no secret and it's not undercover that our God is the Alpha and Omega, the beginning and the end. He is the ultimate manifestation of uniqueness, and none can compare to Him. So as our God is, so we are unique. Please don't misunderstand me—I am not comparing us to the only true and wise God, but trying to show that He loved us so much, He created us with our own special uniqueness.

So, as we live together in this beautiful world of possibilities, we individually bring our uniqueness into opportunities. Just imagine if we brought our uniqueness together with no selfish reasons or cunning, deceitful devices to destroy, no pretense and lies to overcome or get over, but with genuine appreciation for our individual uniqueness.

Can you see it? Your gifts and talents merging with another person's gifts and talents? What a powerful, miraculous union this would be as we appreciate our brothers and sisters for who God created them to be. As we always remember we are just as unique in what has been instilled in us. There would be no place for jealously to reside, so it would have to pack its bags and leave, taking the next jet plane to endlessness.

Never allow someone else to pit you against another person. When you see this type of behavior, take a stand and call it out, whether verbally or silently. With internal silence, you ignore this type of behavior and don't allow it to govern your life. You will find that some people just love confusion and chaos. Walk away and don't look back.

What great things we could accomplish if we saw the bigger picture of future dreams, hopes, and desires through each other's eyes. No big I or little you. We would just allow each other to be who we are—uniquely individual.

There is plenty for all of us to do. But the dilemma at times is, how do I get my arms around this chance called opportunity? What you know for sure is what you adore, which could be your passion, what you are good at, what makes you smile and come alive. What has been burning inside of you? Where do you see a chance to make a difference? For me, it's organizing, coordinating, leading, creating new paths from ground zero, and enjoying my fondness for people. Open your mind and heart, move out of your comfort zone, and make it happen.

The world would be so much better if we recognized what is embedded in each of us. We have individual power to become, but we are individual enough to join and become greater and unified.

We must impart space, provide a platform, pull the curtains back from this stage called life, applaud, and acknowledge each other to Color Our Style! There's room for all of us. Take a step to the right or left and make room for your brothers and sisters as you bow together before the great big audience standing and screaming with excitement, "Encore! Encore!"

We must secure the stage for the next generation of incoming unique color seekers. Help them find their way, guide by example, teach with love, and make sure what is instilled in them is positive. Keep negativity away from their young minds and fill it with unity and wholeness. Be the living example!

They are looking at us. Yes, I'm speaking to the right-now generations. Let's get it right for their sake and give them a head start as one nation under God. Allow them to stand integrated in their uniqueness. Tell them to never be ashamed of who they were created to be—all men are created equal. All can contribute and be genuinely recognized for their contributions. Now, empower yourself and say out loud, "Unleash this uniqueness in me!"

All the colors work together for the good of this nation, for the good of this beautiful world!

An explosion of color!

CONCLUSION

The End of This Journey

At some point in our lives, we will experience the effects of color. Whatever season you may be in, there is a color that relates to your joy, sorrow, pain, hardships, disappointments, and other experiences. But to transition outward and move forward, one must look to another color that draws out promises, new adventures, new opportunities, and brighter expectations. Open your eyes and heart as the colors beckon you to exchange one color for another. You and I must take the first step to change as quoted by

Dr. Martin Luther King Jr: "Faith is taking the first step even when you don't see the whole staircase."

Exchange the brown, desolate ground of the winter season you feel you're standing on as you press through heartaches and pain. Swap it for the summer season of luscious green grass that emerges as a plush mattress to lie down on and take time to rest, replenish, and restore.

Exchange the black, gloomy, sleepless nights brought on by disappointments and loss so you can awaken to the radiance of the bright white sun as it brings a warm hug of encouragement from the prior day. The darkness has delivered its setback; now allow light to engulf and rule the atmosphere.

Exchange the words "I can't go another day" for the calmness of blue skies as birds sing in the new morning and take flight. Now imagine how you can also soar to new heights with a new song of victory: *"I can do all things through Christ who strengthens me"* (Philippians 4:13, NKJV).

Exchange the current color life has you in for a color that can give you a new outlook. Only you can speak life to yourself, encourage yourself, sit in the driver's seat, and defeat the backseat-driver mentality that arises in times when it seems you are allowing others to take full control of your life. And in the times when the backseat driver is you. Yes, you—thinking and speaking defeated messages to yourself.

Remember Deuteronomy 31:6 (MSG): *"Be strong. Take courage. Don't be intimidated. Don't give them a second thought because God, your God, is striding ahead of you. He's right there with you. He won't let you down; he won't leave you."*

Rise higher than your circumstance; go beyond what you see and feel. There's an old hymn that says

The road is rough

The going gets tough

And the hills are hard to climb

But I've decided to make Jesus my choice.

The hymn is telling us we have the authority to decide what choice to make, what direction to take, what path to traverse next. There is a bigger purpose for your life. Look up and live!

As you see, there are so many bold colors of life to choose from. Select one, begin anew, and as you regain your confidence and strength, add more colors, mixing them to create the atmosphere and welcome life for all it has to offer. It will always present some good and bad. But whatever it brings, you can take it and you can make it.

Seek out the color wheel God created and gave freely. Don't allow yourself to stay within the cosmos of one color too long because all colors help mold us and build us to who we are: strong, resilient, powerful, loving, kind, and more. Life experiences may be color-coded for the seasons, but you can rewrite the script and transition to the next level of color, seeing through a new lens to Color Your Style.

Begin to reconnect with yourself through colors and contemplate the following questions. Where do you want to go? What are your ambitions? What are your dreams? What are you passionate about? What are your lifelong goals? Will you allow this situation to defeat you? This is your life, my friend. Do something good with it. Stand and take your place.

When life's challenges knock at your door, it can throw you off the path, but that's the time to see the color in the disruption of what lies ahead on the other side. Freely open the door and face it boldly with confidence, strength, and vigor, determined not to allow it to consume you. No matter what's on the other side—job disappointment, mistreatment, being overlooked, stress, abuse, worry, financial woes—look at it eye to eye, press forward, and become an army of one. Put on the whole armor of God as Ephesians 6:11–17 states, reach for your style color, and get ready for the battle. It's the fight for the finish, the fight for your life that will catapult you to your next level.

See the colors, respect the colors, but most of all honor, adore and give glory to the one who created the colors. Wherever you are, wherever you go, you're covered by the one and only Chief Architect, our Lord and Savior Jesus Christ, and His unconditional love. His love is an umbrella of protection with colors to carry you to the place that is conducive to the life chapter you are facing. Color is here for a reason and not just a season!

So, as we end this journey together, let's plant good seeds of love for the next generation. Seeds that will sprout and be fruitful in any given season. Each generation observes the prior one as they lead the charge for the next one. All are watching, gleaning, and planting the next crop from what they see in our lives. We can make a difference; we must make a difference for their sakes. We cannot continue down the road of exclusion, making up our minds that others are not worthy or having the attitude that the blessings are for me and mine only.

Let's rest assured that we are not in this race alone. There are others who are facing or have faced some of the same challenges, obstacles, and victories in life. Keep in mind Hebrews 12:1–3 (MSG)—allow me to give a short paraphrase here, but go back and read this scripture for yourselves later, pulling out what will encourage you to fight on: There are pioneers and veterans who have blazed the way, cheering us on. Start running and never quit! Keep your eyes on Jesus, who began and finished the race we are in.

We can stop looking at each other as rivals and allow each other to freely come to the table and dine together with our uniqueness, gifts, and talents. Share and live harmoniously on this wonderful planet called Earth, created by the Master Creator who knew exactly how to ensure there was enough room, opportunities, and capacity for all to grow and succeed. He spoke it into existence and it was so, and we can be confident there's enough for all to gather and use to Color Their Style.

Look in the mirror. Make the wise choice not to be ashamed of who you were created to be. God knew just how He wanted you to be before the foundation of the world. My friend, He makes no mistakes. Be proud of your skin color; your freckles; your short or tall stature; your long, straight, wavy, or curly hair; and your slim or slightly larger body. It is who you are. So, cease trying to be like your best friend, sibling, family member, or coworker or the folks in magazines and on TV.

Today we stop allowing others to put us in the box of their vision for us. We stop looking to people to validate our worth. We take charge, write our own vision and make it plain.

Thank you for accompanying me on this journey. I hope the breaks along the trek were enlightening, knowledge-imparting, and instrumental in helping you understand the true essence of this amazing world we live in and the important role through which you contribute to it. I pray you were immersed in the beauty and originality of who you were created to be. You need to fall back in love with you!

So, as we disembark and you gather your personal items, allow me to give one last word of encouragement:

"Here's another way to put it: You're here to be light, bringing out the God-colors in the world. God is not a secret to be kept. We're going public with this, as public as a city on a hill. If I make you light-bearers, you don't think I'm going to hide you under a bucket, do you? I'm putting you on a light stand. Now that I've put you there on a hilltop, on a light stand—shine! Keep open house; be generous with your lives. By opening up to others, you'll prompt people to open up with God, this generous Father in heaven" (Matthew 5:14–16, MSG).

Always remember:

Unique—yes, that's you, and that's me! Believe and be confident there's not another one on this earth quite like you! Your style is you, so color it!

Color My Style

The Canvas

Now it's your turn to build and color your canvas utilizing your creativity and uniqueness. Color Your Style!

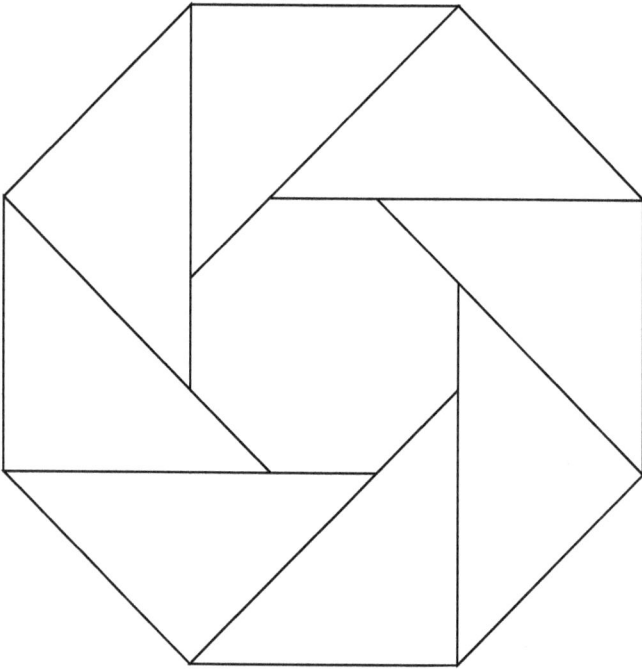

Tag Line Examples

You choose the one that works best to encourage and propel you to the next level.

Color My Style = Uniquely standing!

Color My Style = Uniquely showing up!

Color My Style = Unique and proud!

Color My Style = Bringing forth my best!

Color My Style = Unique, not another like me!

Color My Style = Unique, the one and only!

Color My Style = Embracing my uniqueness!

www.ingramcontent.com/pod-product-compliance
Lightning Source LLC
Chambersburg PA
CBHW071352090426
42738CB00012B/3092